Snow Falling on Chestnut Hill
New and Selected Poems

JOHN F. DEANE was born on Achill Island in 1943. He founded Poetry Ireland – the National Poetry Society – and *The Poetry Ireland Review* in 1978, and is the founder of The Dedalus Press, of which he was editor from 1985 until 2006. In 2008 he was visiting scholar in the Burns Library of Boston College. John F. Deane's poetry has been translated and published in France, Bulgaria, Macedonia, Romania, Italy, Slovakia, Sweden and other countries. His poems in Italian won the 2002 Premio Internazionale di Poesia Città di Marineo. His fiction has been published by Blackstaff Press in Belfast; his most recent novel *Where No Storms Come* was published by Blackstaff in 2011. He is the recipient of the O'Shaughnessy Award for Irish Poetry and the Marten Toonder Award for Literature. John F. Deane is a member of Aosdána, the body established by the Arts Council to honour artists 'whose work had made an outstanding contribution to the arts in Ireland'. His poetry has been shortlisted for the *Irish Times* Poetry Now Award and the T.S. Eliot Prize. In 2007 he was made *Chevalier en l'ordre des arts et des lettres* by the French government. In October 2011 Deane was awarded the Serbian prize: the Golden Key of Smederevo, as well as the Laudomia Bonanni prize from L'Aquila, Italy. He is currently the editor of *Poetry Ireland Review*.

T0099110

Also by John F. Deane from Carcanet Press

Eye of the Hare
A Little Book of Hours
The Instruments of Art
Manhandling the Deity
Toccata and Fugue

JOHN F. DEANE

Snow Falling on Chestnut Hill
New and Selected Poems

CARCANET

Acknowledgements

Parts of some of the pieces in *Snow Falling on Chestnut Hill* have appeared in *PN Review*, *Agenda Magazine*, *Salamander* (USA), *The Poetry Ireland Review*, *Irish Pages*, *The Stinging Fly*, *Southword*, *Image* (USA), *Consequence* (USA; ed. George Kovach), *Voices at the World's Edge* (ed. Paddy Bushe; Dedalus, 2010). Parts were read on the RTÉ Radio programme *Sunday Miscellany*.

First published in Great Britain in 2012 by
Carcanet Press Limited
Alliance House
Cross Street
Manchester M2 7AQ

Text and poem selection copyright © John F. Deane 2012

A CIP catalogue record for this book is available from the British Library
ISBN 978 1 84777 117 9

The publisher acknowledges financial assistance from Arts Council England

Supported by
ARTS COUNCIL
ENGLAND

Printed and bound in England by SRP Ltd, Exeter

Contents

Snow Falling on Chestnut Hill (2012)

SELECTED POEMS

from Toccata and Fugue
(2000)

In Dedication

Under the trees the fireflies
zip and go out, like galaxies;
our best poems, reaching in from the periphery,
are love poems, achieving calm.

On the road, the cries of a broken rabbit
were pitched high in their unknowing;
our vehicles grind the creatures down
till the child's tears are for all of us,

dearly beloved, ageing into pain,
and for herself, for what she has discovered
early, beyond this world's loveliness. Always
after the agitated moments, the search for calm.

Curlews scatter now on a winter field, their calls
small alleluias of survival; I offer you
poems, here where there is suffering and joy,
evening, and morning, the first day.

from TOCCATA AND FUGUE (2000)

Penance

They leave their shoes, like signatures, below;
above, their God is waiting. Slowly they rise
along the mountainside where rains and winds go
hissing, slithering across. They are hauling up

the bits and pieces of their lives, infractions
of the petty laws, the little trespasses and
sad transgressions. But this bulked mountain
is not disturbed by their passing, by this mere

trafficking of shale, shifting of its smaller stones.
When they come down, feet blistered, and sins
fretted away, their guilt remains and that black
mountain stands against darkness above them.

Winter in Meath

To Tomas Tranströmer

Again we have been surprised,
deprived, as if suddenly,
of the earth's familiarity;

it is like the snatching away of love
making you aware at last you loved;

sorrows force their way in, and pain,
like memories half contained;

the small birds, testing boldness,
leave delicate tracks closer
to the back door

while the cherry flaunts blossoms of frost
and stands in desperate isolation.

*

The base of the hedgerow is a cliff of snow,
the field is a still of a choppy sea,
white waves capped in a green spray;

a grave was dug into that hard soil
and overnight the mound of earth
grew stiff and white as stones flung onto a beach.

Our midday ceremony was hurried,
forced hyacinths and holly wreathes dream birds
appearing on our horizonless ocean;

the body sank slowly,
the sea closed over,
things on the seabed
stirred again in expectation.

*

This is a terrible desolation –
the word 'forever' stilling all the air

to glass.

*

Night tosses and seethes;
mind and body chafed all day
as a mussel-boat restlessly
irritates the mooring;

on estuary water a fisherman
drags a long rake against the tide;
one snap of a rope and boat and this
solitary man
sweep off together into night;

perhaps the light from my window
will register a moment with some god
riding by on infrangible glory.

*

At dawn
names of the dead
appear on the pane

beautiful
in undecipherable frost;

breath
hurts them
and they fade.

*

The sea has gone grey as the sky
and as violent;

pier and jetty go under
again and again
as a people suffering losses;

a flock of teal from the world's edge
moves low over the water
finding grip for their wings along the wind;

already, among stones, a man, like a priest,
stooping in black clothes, has begun beachcombing;

the dead, gone silent in their graves,
have learned the truth about resurrection.

*

You can almost look into the sun
silver in its silver-blue monstrance
cold over the barren white cloth of the world;

for nothing happens;

each day is an endless waiting
for the freezing endlessness of the dark;

once – as if you had come across
a photograph, or a scarf maybe –
a silver monoplane like a knife-blade cut
across the still and haughty sky

but the sky healed up again after the passing
that left only a faint, pink thread,
like a scar.

Ghost

I sat where she had sat
in the fireside chair
expecting her to come down the stairs
into the kitchen;

the door was open, welcoming;
coals shifted in the Rayburn,
a kettle hummed,
she heard the susurrations of the fridge;

she had surrounded herself with photographs,
old calendars, hand-coloured picture-postcards;
sometimes a robin looked in at her from the world
or a dog barked vacantly from the hill;

widowed she sat, in the fireside chair,
leaning into a populated past;
she sat so quietly, expecting ghosts,
that a grey mouse moved by, uncurious

till she stomped her foot against the floor;
and did she sense, I wondered, the ghost
who would come after her death to sit
where she had sat, in the fireside chair?

Artist

This was the given image –
a moulded man-body
elongated into pain, the head
sunk in abandonment: the cross;

I see it now
as the ultimate in ecstasy,
attention focused, the final words
rehearsed, there are black

nail-heads and contrasting
plashes of blood
like painter's oils: self-portrait
with grief and darkening sky;

something like Hopkins,
our intent, depressive scholar
who gnawed on the knuckle-bones of words
for sustenance – because God

scorched his bones with nearness
so that he cried with a loud voice
out of the entangling, thorny
underbrush of language.

Christ, with Urban Fox

I

He was always there for our obeisance,
simple, ridiculous,
not sly, not fox, up-front – whatever
man-God, God-man, Christ – but there.
Dreadlocks almost, and girlish, a beard
trim in fashion, his feminine
fingers pointing to a perfect
heart chained round with thorns;
his closed and slim-fine lips
inveigling us towards pain.

II

Did he know his future? while his blood
slicked hotly down the timbers did he know
the great hasped rock of the tomb
would open easily as a book of poems
breathing the words out? If he knew
then his affliction is charade, as is our hope;
if he was ignorant – his mind, like ours,
vibrating with upset – then his embrace of pain
is foolishness beyond thought, and there –
where we follow, clutching to the texts –
rests our trust, silent, wide-eyed, appalled.

III

I heard my child scream out
in pain on her hospital bed,
her eyes towards me where I stood
clenched in my distress;

starched sheets, night-lights, night-fevers,
soft wistful cries of pain,
long tunnel corridors down which flesh
lies livid against the bone.

IV

Look at him now, this king of beasts, grown
secretive before our bully-boy modernity,
master-shadow among night-shadows,
skulking through our wastes. I watched a fox
being tossed under car wheels, thrown like dust
and rising out of dust, howling in its agony;
this is not praise, it is obedience,
the way the moon suffers its existence,
the sky its seasons. Man-God, God-man, Christ,
suburban scavenger – he has danced
the awful dance, the blood-jig, has been strung
up as warning to us all, his snout
nudging still at the roots of intellect.

The Fox-God

Across the fields and ditches, across the unbridgeable
mean width of darkness, a fox barked out its agony;
all night it fretted, whimpering like a famished child,

and the rain fell without pity; it chewed at its flesh,
gnawed on its bared bone, until, near dawn, it died.
The fox, they will say, is vermin, and its god

a vermin god; it will not know, poor creature,
how it is suffering – it is yourself you grieve for.
While I, being still a lover of angels, demanding

a Jacob's ladder beyond our fields, breathed
may El Shaddai console you into that darkness.
I know there was no consolation. No fox-god came.

But at dawn, man the enemy came stalking fields,
snares in his bag, a shotgun cocked. Poor
creatures. The gap out of life, we have learned,

is fenced over with affliction. We, too, some dusk,
will take a stone for pillow, we will lie down, snared,
on the uncaring earth. Poor creatures. Poor creatures.

The Taking of the Lambs

The ewes were shifting in the darkness,
exhaling sorrow in wooden
dunts of incomprehension; lightning
skittered on the horizon,
the milky way
was a vast meandering sheep-track;

the gate was barred again
and the hard hooves of the ewes
slithered in the glaur,
their legs too thin tonight to sustain
the awful weight of their bodies;

the sheep-dogs stretched, contented,
soon to be swore at again,
curmudgeoned and cringing
and the dung-stained truck
loomed in the yard; night

seemed the shadow of a maker God
laid down over the world,
and even the stars in their obedience
stepped out their side-shuffle dance
of destruction, the thunder
eventually rolling down.

Fugue

1. THE EXPERIENCE OF WHAT IS BEAUTIFUL

(i)

The ships move down at evening on waters
flowing out of Knowth and Dowth and Newgrange;
they glide along our fields with fixed high lights
electrifying dusk; out past the lighthouse
the ocean sways with the swing of the stars;
you stand at the doorway, hear the iron
heartbeat, are hurt with longing; ours
the order of the underearth, of darkness
gathering off the horizon; you shut the door
sensing again in the confines of the house
the ever-pressing burden of your affliction.

You would put everything within reach
into your mouth; I want to tell you – *let it be*;
in the labour ward you forced eyes open
against the birth-flood, witnessing already
our sad condition, our brute
necessities; the sorrow began that begins
at birth, you opening your mouth
to scream as if you would devour the earth
and – *let it be* – I wanted to tell you – *just
let it be*, but: watchful, scared, I
hesitated, having my angers too, my appetites.

The hares sit stolidly in the mist at dawn;
you may refuse to see how lovely they appear,
familiar, like the recently dead who stroll
speaking and gesticulating amongst themselves
under the glistening leaves of the sycamores,
holding you with their indifference, needing you
to flesh them out though you walk right through them
– as through the glistering cobwebs on the ferns –
and out on the factory road. They have gone now,

the hares; in their place the burden of another day,
its necessary structures, its lethargies.

The sun through frosted windows gleamed
like sea-lights on a high suspended crucifix;
angels like water-birds perched on the muscles
of his arms, their heads the skulls of famished
children staring on our shores with wonder;
you lit a candle and watched the flame
quivering, your fingers trembling with delight;
I brushed your hand along the smooth veneer
of the coffin-timbers, said the word you could not
understand: *adieu*, the woodgrain beautiful
as if high tides left ripples on its sand.

You sit, in failing light, on the carpet;
if I press this switch the light comes on –
do you know that yet? If you listen
you'll hear the taut strings of the piano
play pressure-music; in a sudden tantrum
you knock the tower you have painstakingly
built; you will learn there is no happiness
unchained to cause and consequence but I
can only sweep you up and quiet you; the music
the piano holds, the *Pathétique*, has been played
on it so often it is a memory in its gut.

I could speak, from my innocence, of God, and you
refuse to hear me. See how the river moves
always at our side, swollen in the estuary
at measurable times; the whooper swans
fly over, following directions given
thousands of years ago, their bodies freighted
with vegetative energy; we number them, and note
how their wings drum rhythms on the air, how their calls
are the flute-music of a score till I believe
in an ordering God to which we may aspire; the swans,
with sighing sounds, wheel in unison towards the reeds.

This is not how it was intended,
to follow down your mother's tracks,
hurt and stumbling; abandoning
all we had built together is not
what you ought to do with your life.

There were times we sang to God
in the old church on the shoreline,
touched the beautiful together:
sloblands, estuary waters,
cormorants with their wings out

drying in the sun, still as nuns
in noontime meditation; we saw
slime-covered rocks, factory excreta
miring the channel walls;
we tested echoes in the church,

traced coloured moths of light
until we knew that only the real
is beautiful, and only the beautiful
is real. But there was this
child, born reluctantly a girl, willing

to reject at once the given,
as if the moment of conception came
a fraction early, or a fraction late.
I carried you to the factory, galvanise
dangled from a girder and scratched

stubbornly against itself in the breeze;
they ground fish-bones here, fish-heads,
the stench of long-decayed sea-things
bathed us; and this, too, is beautiful,
because it is, because it is.

2. EVENING, MIDNIGHT, COCK-CROW, DAWN

You would devour the world, as the moguls do,
    their six-day wars, their desert storms;
I pray sometimes for the Christ
    to tear open the heavens and come down!

I have been withering like leaves, longing –
    like a wind – has been blowing me about.

I started out along the streets
    in debilitating fog; you'd be afraid these years …

The maul of traffic, abstracted people
    reduced again to basic needs;
shopwindows with little sign of the Child,
    commerce only, and passing profit;

I longed to hear, as I turned
    into the cloister garth, the strong
tenor voice call out:
    comfort ye!

*

I moved listlessly about the house today
    seething at emptiness;
if I could rid myself of expectation,
    translate old faith into new realities –
I have been patient, awake and watchful,
    evening, midnight, cock-crow, dawn,

to discover only your shadow, darkening.
    Snow on the high reaches
sang beneath us as we walked;
    our breath formed shapes and disappeared;
nothing on earth
    can be the object of your desire.

You pass along the estuary road, wearing
    a walkman, your head
a labyrinthine underground
    with jangling escalators, iron stairs:
rap, new fangle, ego-trippin';
    'turkey makes it a real Christmas';

a snipe
    zipped suddenly from the grass,
flicked preciously away –
    but you are turned in
onto yourself, the volume up, and truth
    hurtling from you into the air.

I have lost strength now and only wait,
    unhopeful, hurt by your hurting.
Over the fields a carpeting of frost,
    your footsteps, fleeing, left a sad
black slither-trail behind you;
    we have laid ourselves

down along a hedge like old enamel basins
    waiting to be made beautiful with snow;
I would stand, a larch, under the weight of frost
    weather-patient, desiring (hard thing!)
what God desires and be
    mindless, unanxious, whole.

*

We have settled at last into the harmonics;
    around us the effigies, brasses, plaques,
the weight of a difficult history,
    and the ghost – that sour Dean

quieted a while;
    out of the wilderness of a stilled heart
may glory break: Be
    still. Listen. Be at peace.

*

Advents flare, go out; tinsel bells hang stiff
    on tinsel trees;
we prepare, in mourning purple, for a birth,
    rehearsing our parts in the mystery;

the seasonal romping hymns
    have been pedalled out and the old,
unsullied manger: for unto us a Child …
    I remember you, small, still awed,

your big, unwieldy glasses;
    you knelt on the marble step
your body innocent with wonder;
    when he does come, that adult child,

it will be agony to sullied flesh,
    it will be fire along the structures of the brain
as if a life were straw; this
    is not our season, who have begun to age.

3. DANCE OF THE HOURS (MODERATO)

They are teaching you the clock, how to tell
time: an old man's face, two fingers
pointing; and other
sing-song things till the world begins to fill

with the future, purposes for your still-slight
self. Night comes early now,
tail-lights are poison berries
against the black-green foliage of night;

it is the rhythmic fall and lift,
Gregorian chant of stars and seasons,
miracles of obedience
I point you to, the epiphanic gifts

of redwing, fieldfare, the godwit's sound.
Morning, cars furred with frost;
we water them and they breathe out like cattle
turning cautiously onto difficult ground;

we would sleep this harshest season through
wrapped in ourselves like bears, dreaming
of fuchsia, apple blossom, bees.
I gathered you from school,

we stood on the bridge to watch a train
crescendo from the south;
you put your hands to your ears and screamed
as it rushed beneath and died away

towards the north; sleeper after sleeper, stave-notes,
the self needs purposes
of past and future. Come
from the bridge; you are young yet

in the music, a dead mother
will be a difficult life-partner; at the high
spiked gates out of childhood you pluck
the frets of a badly-tuned guitar,

your song yourself, false
notes, disaster-chords. Near home the river
deepens before the sea; through black depths
like a Bach cantata the water flows;

on the mud-flats a black-iron boiler lies
deep in slob. Home at last we lit
a wax candle for the man who has died,
that stubbled face, those aqueous humoured eyes,

reader in the testament of pain.
A full moon leans over the parishes, bathes
the marsh-fields, glaur and mud-daub
in an alabaster glow; we flow through time

note by impossible note, out
towards eternity;
the old man's face,
the fingers, pointing; and the candle lit

for old time's sake,
for what has happened
and goes on happening, for our
unfathomable days.

4. THE MARSH ROAD

He taught me God, without insisting, loved me,
as I love you, through hurt, beyond;
and God became all gentleness, a life.
We dug for worms in the vegetable field;
he stooped over the spade in concentration,

they uncoiled coiled about each other
in his tin tobacco box; we sat together
on the riverbank, patient and watching,
close to the pulsing by of the world.
To be pierced like that and hung midstream,

out of the natural element! so that now my mind
revolts at it, revolts too at the face that peers
absorbed over its purposes –
his gentle hands drawing the fleshly shape
over the hook like a glove, we two hunched

in voluntary cruelty – and I saw God too
lean leering out over the rim of the world,
absorbed. I have tried to urge that love
be the motive that supplies your energy
but you walk away from me on the marsh road,

your walkman drowning out my calls.
I watched him, stooped at last over himself,
sitting in the ward, alone, and absent;
he was labouring to admit God's hands
drawing his flesh onto pain like a glove,

suspended in the gullet between life and death;
I could not intrude, I prayed him grace
and he came back wearied from his far country;
it was the dying of the old man, the ego
hung midstream, out of the natural element.

We are, as if we are forever; our passage
will be difficult; when it comes at last
that we are other, dumb and senseless,
presiding out of photographs or from a book,
the terrible angel at the gate will ask of us

what we have done for the gratification of the world.
Can you accept death in advance of death?
Can you accept the Christ, though he is dead,
may walk our streets, disheartened, jostled,
or out along the marsh-road, calling and ignored?

5. PATHÉTIQUE

(i)

Once it begins there is no …
        And it began.
You were trollied.
        Tested. Soothed.

The way of pain is through the spine, along
        the swift streaming of the blood.
Affliction
        marrows the skeleton, inflames

the mind.
        A legacy. Wolf-
cub; out of
        darkness ... Such

suffering ought not to be. But is.
        Struggle
fiercely against it. Struggle
        to become

light. You walked
        disconsolately down the long corridor and turned
out of our holding.
        They drew

curtains round your bed;
        we stood in the corridor, waiting;
they were murmuring together
        a long time.

The *pietà*. In the other's face
        the all of human suffering has been stilled
to a pool, watchful; the
        wolf-Christ, the

mother. Once
        you were merriest of us all; I root
in my overcoat's deep pockets for strength.
        You,

wakeful, sweating,
       the night orderly
down in the dayroom,
       reading.

                    (ii)

    And there you are suddenly, after all,
running into rain and darkness, as if to gain
       distance from yourself and the demands of love,
carrying your burden with you
       into the ditches and doorways, skulking;

you are the fox in the rusted snare
       eating through his bone to escape
the hand that would release him.
       Snowdrops have appeared
among the trodden grasses, something

       urging itself again towards life;
we have warmed ourselves by winter fires,
       carried ashes out in supermarket bags, but
your complicity in your pain
       leaves the world with grey-black embers

colder than any cold;
       this is in-country suffering, no hope
of the broad horizons of the sea; you
       in the night, in the high cabin
of a juggernaut, grown anonymous,

       laying your life down pendant, breathless.
How the world, at man's whim, becomes
       a dumb thing, subject only
to the laws of rainfall and the drift
       of sludge; how we butcher in our time

the gentle, wide-eyed seals,
        drive shafts into the quick
of the pensive whale, insinuate
        nuclear dust into the air about us; you
running from the door into embracing darkness.

        Midnight over, the police car
entering the estates, bringing you
        furtively, back; animal thing
huddled, wet and cold, on the concrete floor,
        cradling grief to you like a broken fox.

6. THE FULLNESS OF DESIRE

(i)

In the dead days of the year we celebrated birth;
in spring we are labouring towards a death;
inelegant spirals of flies dance in the sun,

lambs in the corners of our fields pick their first steps
towards slaughter; all of us creatures, poor creatures,
exulting when we can, in our matter.

You have been dwindling towards darkness,
found yourself a corner with a few childish things
about you, leaving the world beyond high walls.

Necessity, I long to tell you, is brute;
how they loaded creels on the donkey's back,
how they rode his rump and thumped his ribs

and never thought. We will not learn! the boulders
shriek at our disobedience, who set ourselves apart
as small arbitrary gods; the donkey

stands for hours against rain, donkey-absent,
his manifold complaint perfectly contained
until the shuddering bray releases it

to air. Somewhere out in natural darkness
a man is whistling up his dog; expose yourself again
to light. We came in through the high gates;

magpies strutted on the lawns and cornices;
inside are the halls of mirrors, heavy with smoke
and sadness, with coffee and biscuit dreams;

your days are spent rehearsing
illusions of autonomous existence;
other shades, your neighbours, shuffle –

rouged and pearled – along these
urine-smelling streets, as if they had a purpose.
You turn away. We have lost you. You are satisfied.

(ii)

Innocence went abroad
in short trousers; we trooped
to collect His signature:

ashes corked on the brow
in the shape of a grey-smudged
cross; third eye; but we were

generous in fasting, grew
lean as a furze bush; I among
grey-dun hillsides, sea

and street and hedgerow all
obedient unto death; blessed
sacrament; necessity's child;

the world was neat and headlined,
enclosed within the fragrant
store-house of a schoolbag,

between corn-flake-packet covers
the printed word, and everything
imprimatur; point

A to Z, obey! like
salley-rods, like rodents, like slime-
slick eels in the quarry lake.

(iii)

Mist in the forenoon; cattle shifting
languorously, their wet eyes watching;
over the fields hung Good Friday mystery;

we stood about, waiting; a hare, big bucko,
sat attentive; surviving buckshot, his kind
has grown fluid in the arts of living.

We had gathered after a death; big men,
naturally sure among the animals, shifted
awkward with suits, awkward with belief;

the coffin had been received, he will go down
wearing a fine blood-rose in his lapel.
They have gone home now, honey-lights on the altar

have been quenched; do you remember –
in the age of innocence – the stations? how we went
round slowly in the lugubrious dance, the

Stabat Mater, flectamus genua; how we knew
we had generosity and love to lift us
somewhere between earth and heaven?

The altar has been stripped for the ceremony;
the rest of the day will be coloured purple;
I kneel in a dim cave of silence; the man,

moved to a side aisle, has found repose;
there is the soft creak of benches, pale light
palely filtered, the hidden sun will set early;

nothing miraculous to be expected; what is demanded
is the obedience of stillness, the slaking of thirst
with bitterness, the prolonged suffering that is love.

Attend. Be faithful. Grow fluid. Be at peace.

from Manhandling the Deity
(2003)

Officium

Spare me Lord for my days burn off like dew.
What is man that you should magnify him;
why do you tender towards him your heart of love?
You visit him at dawn, touching him with dreams,
whisper to him at dusk, while the swings still shift
and soft rain falls on the abandoned frames.
Why have you made him contrary to you
that he learn baseness, anger and defeat
swallowing his own saliva in sudden dread?
Can you erase his sins, like chalk marks,
or place your angels as a fence about him?
The trees dreep softly, the attendants are gone home.
Today I will lie down in sand, and if tomorrow
you come in search of me, I am no more.

Frenzy

A small row-boat on Keel Lake,
the water sluppering gently as he rowed,
the easy sh-sh-sshhhh of the reeds

as we drifted in, and all about us
tufts of bog-cotton like white moths,
the breathing heathers, that green-easy lift

into the slopes of Slievemore. All else
the silence of islands, and the awe
of small things wonderful: son,

father, on the one keel, the ripples
lazy and the surfaces of things unbroken.
Then the prideful swish of his line

fly-fishing, the curved rod graceful,
till suddenly mayfly were everywhere,
small water-coloured shapes like tissue,

sweet as the host to trout and – *by Jove!*
he whispered, old man astounded again
at the frenzy that is in all living.

Nightwatch

In our suburban villages, our dormitory towns
we lie secure. But at the city's core
up and down the crack-tiled steps of the men's
shelter, they pass who could be minister

or president or priest – but are not;
in dust-striped suits and mismatched waistcoats
who could be civil servants – but are not;
greased and creased and ill at ease they ghost,

side-staggering, our streets, who might
be Plato, Luther, Hopkins but for some tiny thing
that slipped and shifted them a little to the side.
Their dream is a coin found under slanting

light, oblivion enough to damp down care
a while. But wish us all good health and reason
who wake sometimes, knowing we too have been
visited by importunate ghosts and have forgotten;

tell us what we dreamed, interpret for us the dream.

Matrix

I took the pollack, fat from his predations
round the roots of the black rocks
and flopping now on the cliff ledge

and flung him high –

he shaped an arc of ecstacy through the air,
near-dead fish flying, and whooped
back again into the sea of love.

The Book of Love

Perhaps the words of poems
I am writing for you now
may drift before your consciousness
(long after you and I are ghosts)
like something almost assuming
shape out of the long misting
of a long and misty day,
gone already but sustaining
among eternity's shiftless constellations:
that you and I have loved one another
across the in-between slow-motion times
we did not note exceptional, but were
the steadily sustaining everyday
alphabet of our togetherness.

from MANHANDLING THE DEITY (2003)

House Martins

Their round heads butting from the nest
they were three –
cowled and fledgling monks,
or novice topers with elbows
resting along the bar,
plump already and demanding,
the clean stillness of their egging
dumped.

Their nest was a miracle of mud and bird-spittle,
fastened like the church of Rome
to the highest niche available,
the world beneath them
despicable in soil and bird-shit –

but oh how the adults waltzed and tangoed down the air,
each one
a muscle perfected into flight,
impelled and catapulted to wear out
the sweetest season of their summering into care.

Soon
they will have fled the nest, a little
groggily, but proud as prelates, and you know again
in the secret place within that houses grace,
that everything beyond the rule and filthying of men
is whole, and holy, and unsoiled.

Acolyte

The wildness of this night – the summer trees
ripped and letting fall their still green leaves,
and the sea battering the coast
in its huge compulsion – seems as nothing

to the midnight chime from the black tower,
reiterating that all this tumult
is but the bones of Jesus in their incarnation.
I have flown today onto the island,

our small plane tossed like jetsam on the clouds;
I watched the girl, her mutilated brain,
the father urging, how her body rocked
in unmanageable distress, her fingers

bruising a half-forgotten doll; hers, too,
the Jesus-body, the Jesus-bones. Once
in early morning, the congregation
was an old woman coughing against echoes

and a fly frantic against the high window;
the words the priest used were spoken out as if
they were frangible crystal: *hoc – est – enim* …
The Host was a sunrise out of liver-spotted hands

and I tinkled the bell with a tiny gladness;
the woman's tongue was ripped, her chin,
where I held the paten, had a growth of hairs;
her breath was fetid and the Host balanced

a moment, and fell. Acolyte I gathered
up the Deity, the perfect white of the bread
tinged where her tongue had tipped it; the
necessary God, the beautiful, the patience.

I swallowed it, taking within me
Godhead and congregation, the long obedience
of the earth's bones, and the hopeless urge
to lay my hands in solace on the world.

Gotland, July 2000

Fantasy in White

Over the brimming acres of wild meadow
the white butterflies, in a silent storm
of winged snowflakes, were fluttering
through their extravagant mating dance;
in this our fractured time and world-space
those of us who know ourselves to be broken
rejoiced in a moment of purest wonder;
where sin abounds there grace abounds the more.
By evening, absence had settled on the meadow
as after the exhalation of a deep-drawn breath,
one high star chilling in a grey, bleak sky;
imperceptibly the fall had come
and we turned once more towards the dark,
the white soul weighted in its winter boots.

The Apotheosis of Desire

(Luke Ch. 7: 'And behold a woman who was a sinner in the city … who came and stood behind at his feet, weeping. And she began to bathe his feet with her tears, and wiped them with her hair …')

I

The motorway, pre-dawn, in sickly light;
a cruel misting of spray from night-travelling
articulated trucks; the stomach clenching; a fox
crossed before my lowered lights, its lovely wildness
undiminished. The airport was its own city

in a haze of lights. Everywhere we move we move
with shadows; empty escalators roll
with an iron muttering; coffee machines stand bright,
untempting. When we go on board, at last, we go
like pilgrims already weary. The runways, at dawn,

are wood-paths with bauble-lights. Soon
we are high into quickening sunlight, as if ignorant again
that underneath is another world more real, and less,
than this. I pray: that his hand
bear you safely over the abyss until you land

on that loveliest of shores. Our cruciform shadow
shifting on the clouds below, is haloed in rainbows;
we are eight miles high – the ascending Christ
would have been lost to view, ice
taking his Jewish beard and being. The high life,

whiskey, pretzels; ice cubes clinking in the glass.

II

I am defiled, frustrated by desire.
There were some attended to his words
to pick among them afterwards, like daws;

I consented, simply, without having understood.
God's are the domains of mystery, mine
the concerns of longing, the domains of flesh.

Now the frenzy of living has been set aside,
the frenzy of dying anticipated, my life
trapped amongst high-tide refuse. I am all

attention; vulnerable soul-flesh; out of shell.
I had heard the name, rumours, marvels, bastard; what
understanding could be possible? Save that he

consented to my being, as I to his.
I was hopeless for him, the longing
numbed as when I stood outside his tomb, despondent.

I sit in darkness, waiting; a flame
burns in the glass, lights my absorption, as if my hand
cupped a cold, smooth skull; I would flay my flesh

in punishment, but for the worth of my still black hair
and the pathos of male cravings. He loved me, too,
I saw, for a time, beyond both flame and darkness;

and what have I to show? Old bones knotted.

III

After years this, today, is the found land, this
the old tome of marvels, the debilitating life-ache.
A solitary boy, Jew-child, plays apart, his ball
thunking down the stone steps from the Rock;
a lizard, like a spill of oil, flicks itself

into a crevice as I shift under the heat. The Old City
is a sea in storm, history a stone ship, I find
little I can cling to. *It's Jihad*, Tibi said, *rules
are down, and listen! our orders come direct from God*;
there are funerals in Ramallah, and women wailing

out of Beit Jala, the smaller children gathering stones
for sling-shots. Here you can rent a cross of smoothly
planed wood; among the confusion of gods I find
tourist signs pointing the Via Dolorosa; I step
cautiously over my dreams, find kitsch, the Coca-Cola signs,

the overwhelming smell of spices and naked meat,
stalls rife with the junk of old piosity. Bring
your signature, your banker's card. If I could touch
something he had touched, some trace that he had stepped
on original clay. I stand back among the shadows,

wipe sweat from my brow, find little comfort.

IV

We sat quietly on the wooden pier, lake water
lulling us. My head on his shoulder, his right hand
around me, left hand in mine. He turned, asking

'What are you thinking? Tell me.' And between
what I had been thinking, and the putting of it into words
was devastating territory I could not cross.

Out over the lake the sorrow-laden flight
of the flamingos; mallard were in dispute among the reeds,
a solitary heron, angular, discrete, stood near shore.

I was in love, and scared. He, too, was scared, violent
agitation and territories occupied; funerals in Ramallah
and women wailing. Man is flesh, the spirit

will not remain in him forever. I followed him;
I saw his blood dreep down onto the clay; I heard him scream
in agony and despair, like I do, inwardly. I listen

to footsteps of the pious go shush across the temple floor. I held
his flesh once more, dawn, blue-sky and virginal, the tomb
door open, but he urged me from him, into shadows. Now I touch

the cold stones in the Western Wall, remembering
the rush and wildness once of his love, wondering
what can my life give back to Christ for this my life.

Oh devious God, dweller in shadows, mercy on us, the afflicted.

V

They laid him on his mother's knees, like an old child,
face distorted, and slow dribbles of blood
along his Jewish beard; I touched the perfect quarter-moons

of his fingernails, the lifeline like a contour map of the sky.
She and I, silenced, holding the hurt back, the way you hold
your palm to your side to contain the suffering.

I had washed my tears into his feet, the bitterness
of renounced possession, human love prefiguring
death; I dried them with my hair; the devils in me

the violent eroticism of my love. They had handled him
with violence, their scourges, lances, nails; I loved him,
how can I then forgive, or be forgiven?

I make my way sometimes up that dirt track
where people jostled for a view; stones, his naked feet,
the gouts of blood that made a paste against the clay. Desire

has been an overwhelming force within me; now
I am a pigeon home to roost on a soiled window ledge.
I attend. They will bury me with those tight-packed

inside the crevices on the hill, my heart's desire
shrivelled to an olive stone. So much love
has been written out with a stick on the dry earth

waiting for the winds to whistle it away.

VI

We have set it up so often, remembering, on the rough
wood of the cross, the body, bared. I came, seeking
the Jesus-body, the Jesus-bones. In the Church of the Holy
                                                    Sepulchre
someone was playing Bach, softly: *Jesu joy*
of man's desiring ... I stood in awe; candles about the tomb,

Madonna lilies high and innocent; this, at last,
is the centre of creation; from here
he lies to north and south, he lies to east
and west and is the compass in me and the draw, it is in him
ultimately, I will be earthed. I have been handling

only my own desires, and walk again, uncertain.
Between the crevices of the Western Wall, paper slips
hold prayers that make a mortar of human pleading.
The onion domes of the Church of St Mary Magdalene
stand certain against the sky on the Mount of Olives;

I thought of her, would speak with her, of that
virginal morning, that shifting, uncertain shadow.
A vapour trail passed, slowly, high across the perfect blue.
And then frenzy again, of airports. Star-flights. Half-sleep.
Pre-dawn and my own familiar coastline, the plane

shuddering in storm as we came back down to earth.

Canticle

Sometimes when you walk down to the red gate
hearing the scrape-music of your shoes across gravel,
a yellow moon will lift over the hill;
you swing the gate shut and lean on the topmost bar
as if something has been accomplished in the world;
a night wind mistles through the poplar leaves
and all the noise of the universe stills
to an oboe hum, the given note of a perfect
music; there is a vast sky wholly dedicated
to the stars and you know, with certainty,
that all the dead are out, up there, in one
holiday flotilla, and that they celebrate
the fact of a red gate and a yellow moon
that tunes their instruments with you to the symphony.

from The Instruments of Art
(2005)

Late October Evening

We sat and watched the darkness close
– like a slow galleon under black sail
nearing; and grew conscious again of those
of our loved dead who might come, pale

in their murmuring group, up the long road
towards us. Thrush and blackbird hurled
valiant songs against the gloom as though
this was the first dying of the world.

You and I drew closer still
in the fire's glow, grateful this far
for love and friendship, while the low hill
melded with the dark and a perfect star

swung on its shoulder. When I turned back,
near sleep, to hold you, I could pray
our dead content again under black
sails, the tide brimming, then falling away.

from THE INSTRUMENTS OF ART (2005)

The Gift

And did you catch it then? That offered flash
of brilliance across the gloom? There by a curve
of the river, by the salleys and ash-trees, a brash
iridescence of emerald and blue –
kingfisher! Skulking you were, and sulking, astray
from sacrament and host, with your dreary
dwelling on the ego. Pathetic. Pray
grace in that sacred presentation, the high
shock of what is beautiful leading you to betray
this self-infusion for a while. And then that cry –
its piping *chee-chee-chee*, secretive by the stream's drift
and you step closer, cautiously, grace being still
easily squandered, till you have it before you: the gift!
Loveliness, and a dagger-like poised bill.

The Meadows of Asphodel

The gate leans crookedly and blue binding-twine
clamps it against strays. Over peat acres
bog-cotton sways like a chorus of souls arrayed

for paradise, prepared to utter into praise.
In this humped meadow the individual graves
are clothed in dogrose and montbretia, clumps

of soiled-white lilies and the tut-tut-tutting
wheatears. Neglect, I say, and you say
repose, how the dead have abandoned us, become

seeds curled in darkness, their only task to wait
the nourishment and ripening; here it is the living
are blown about by the winds. The stones

with their weathering, their burthen of names
and aspirations, face, you say, all in the same
direction, and I say, East, waiting

for that disturbance, the grincing of the gate
when we will all stir out of repose, and lift, prepared
for counting, like pale down shivering before the breeze.

Adagio Molto

I see them, Father, Son and feminine Spirit,
through the nothingness of space and absence,
in a passionate passacaglia, happy to be getting
nowhere; creating, in repose,
harmony, time, the rhythm of the seasons.

And I see the girl, young still in the soul's
heavenward journey, gravity and grace in her decorum,
standing obedient to the forces of clay and cloud that make
Vivaldi: *Gloria*
in excelsis Deo, fingers of the left hand

alert with wisdom, the right dictatorial, commanding
the winds and waves of the prayer. She, also,
passionate and at work, like this window-cleaner –
questions, too, of gravity and grace –
who hangs by threads at the twenty-seventh floor,

sheening glass to a metaphor of clouds
in a high, unblemished sky. Sounds from the world
are rumour merely, and it will not be easy –
in terra pax – to come down
and walk once more among the citizens.

The Instruments of Art

Edvard Munch

We move in draughty, barn-like spaces, swallows
busy round the beams, like images. There is room
for larger canvases to be displayed, there are storing-places
for our weaker efforts; hold

to warm clothing, to surreptitious nips of spirits
hidden behind the instruments of art. It is all, ultimately,
a series of bleak self-portraits, of measured-out
reasons for living. Sketches

of heaven and hell. Self-portrait with computer;
self-portrait, nude, with blanching flesh; self
as Lazarus, mid-summons, as Job, mid-scream.
There is outward

dignity, white shirt, black tie, a black hat
held before the crotch; within, the turmoil, and advanced
decay. Each work achieved and signed announcing itself
the last. The barn door slammed shut.

*

There was a pungency of remedies on the air, the house
hushed for weeks, attending. A constant focus
on the sick-room. When I went in, fingers reached for me,
like crayfish bones; saliva

hung in the cave of the mouth like a web. Later,
with sheets and eiderdown spirited away, flowers stood
fragrant in a vase in the purged room. Still life. Leaving
a recurring sensation of dread, a greyness

like a dye, darkening the page; that *Dies Irae*, a slow
fretsaw wailing of black-vested priests. It was Ireland
subservient, relishing its purgatory. Books, indexed,
locked in glass cases. Night

I could hear the muted rhythms in the dance-hall; bicycles
slack against a gable-wall; bicycle-clips, minerals, the raffle;
words hesitant, ill-used, like groping. In me the dark bloom
of fascination, an instilled withdrawal.

                        *

He had a long earth-rake and he drew lines
like copy-book pages on which he could write
seeds, meaning – love; and can you love, be loved, and never
say 'love', never hear 'love'?

The uncollected apples underneath the trees
moved with legged things and a chocolate-coloured rust;
if you speak out flesh and heart's desire will the naming of it
canker it? She cut hydrangeas,

placed them in a pewter bowl (allowing herself at times
to cry) close by the tabernacle door; patience in pain
mirroring creation's order. The boy, suffering puberty, sensed
in his flesh a small revulsion, and held

                        *

hands against his crotch in fear. Paint the skin
a secret-linen white with a smart stubble of dirt. The first
fountain-pen, the paint-box, pristine tablets of Prussian Blue,
of Burnt Sienna – words

sounding in the soul like organ-music, Celeste and Diapason –
and that brush-tip, its animated bristles; he began at once
painting the dark night of grief, as if the squirrel's tail
could empty the ocean onto sand. Life-

drawing, with naked girl, half-light of inherited faith,
colour it in, and rhyme it, blue. In the long library, stooped
over the desks, we read cosmology, the reasoning
of Aquinas; we would hold

the knowledge of the whole world within us. The dawn
chorus: *laudetur Jesus Christus*; and the smothered,
smothering answer: *in aeternum. Amen.* Loneliness
hanging about our frames, like cassocks. New

*

world, new day. It is hard to shake off darkness, the black
habit. The sky at sunset – fire-red, opening its mouth
to scream; questions of adulthood, exploration of the belly-flesh
of a lover. It was like

the rubbling of revered buildings, the moulding of words
into new shapes. In the cramped cab of a truck she, first time,
                                                    fleshed
across his knees; the kiss, two separate, not singular,
alive. It was death already, prowling

at the dark edge of the wood, fangs bared, saliva-white.
Sometimes you fear insanity, the bridge humming to your scream
(oil, casein, pastel) but there is nobody to hear, the streaming river
only, and the streaming sky; soon

on a dark night, the woman tearing dumbly at her hair while you
gaze uselessly onto ashes. Helpless again you fear
woman: saint and whore and hapless devotee. Paint your words
deep violet, pale yellow,

*

the fear, *Winter in Meath, Fugue, the Apotheosis of Desire.*
The terror is not to be able to write. Naked and virginal
she embraced the skeleton and was gone. What, now,
is the colour of *God is love*

when they draw the artificial grass over the hole, the rains
hold steady, and the diggers wait impatiently under trees? Too long
disturbing presences were shadowing the page, the bleak
ego-walls, like old galvanise

round the festering; that artificial mess collapsing
down on her, releasing a small, essential spirit, secular
bone-structure, the fingers reaching out of *need*, no longer *will*.
Visceral edge of ocean,

wading things, the agitated ooze, women on the jetty
watching out to sea; at last, I, too, could look
out into the world again. The woman, dressed in blue, broke
from the group on the jetty and came

*

purposefully towards us, I watched through stained glass of the door,
and loved her. Mine the religion of poetry, the poetry
of religion, the worthy Academicians unwilling to realise
we don't live off neglect. Is there

a way to understand the chaos of the human heart? our
slaughters, our carelessness, our unimaginable wars?
Without a God can we win some grace? Will our canvases,
their patterns and forms, their

rhymes and rhythms, supply a modicum of worth?
The old man dragged himself up the altar steps,
beginning the old rites; the thurible clashed against its chain;
we rose, dutifully, though they

have let us down again, holding their forts
against new hordes; I had hoped the canvas would be filled
with radiant colours, but the word God became a word
of scorn, easiest to ignore. We

*

came out again, our heartache unassuaged.
The high corral of the Academy, too, is loud with gossipers,
the ego-traffickers, nothing to be expected there. Self-
portrait, with grief

and darkening sky. Soon it will be the winter studio; a small
room, enclosed; you will sit, stilled, on a wooden chair, tweed
heavy about your frame, eyes focused inwards, where there is
no past, no future; you sit alone,

your papers in an ordered disarray; images stilled, like nests
emptied; the phone beside you will not ring; nor will the light
come on; everything depends on where your eyes
focus; when

the darkness comes, drawing its black
drape across the window, there will remain
the stillness of paint, words on the page, the laid down
instruments of your art.

The Study

Over the deal table a flower-patterned oil-cloth;
the boy
has his Bible history open before him; its pictures

of deserts, and of stylised heroes of God's militias;
he is chewing on a pencil-end
as if hunger for knowledge frustrates him and he spits

small splinters out onto the stone-flagged floor;
outside
hydrangeas are in bloom, their sky-blue flowers

big as willow-pattern plates; on the kitchen wall
a picture of Jesus, stylised,
fingers long as tapers, ringlets honey-brown, and eyes

lifted querulously towards the ceiling;
a red, eternal light
flickers weakly below the picture;

but the saddened eyes have lowered, and peer
down on the restless
stooped-over boy, in anger or in mute and trenchant

pleading;
and only a summer bee
distraught against the window, makes any sound.

You

I am sea-born, and sea-inclined; islanded
on this earth, dragged each-which-way, and tidal;

senses shifting as the sands shift, my soul
flotsam. Prisoned in time, and you, love,

are eternity, you are the current in my depths,
my promised shore. And when I part from you,

taking my words to dry, sophisticated places, I am
tugged towards you, sweet desperation, this underwater storm.

Carnival of the Animals

Someone played piano in a far room: scales
growing out of black earth, blossoming, and falling back.

*

From outside, a cock's
hilarious response, all his hens
busily indifferent to his brass ego, indifferent too
to the honed axe-blade, waiting in the dark outhouse.

*

Badger, noon-time, after his night
hours of raids and rhapsodies,
roadside lies in dust, the stench of his decay
ghosting already on leaf and mayflower.

*

Cat comes, secretly, to the lupin-beds
to dream, will leave
bruised warm spaces, cat-sweet, like dreams; and big
bucko the hare comes lolloping through the wild meadow
to chew on the salt new leaves of the rose-bush;

*

for a moment, attendant on what is beautiful, I forgot myself.
But someone called from a far room: *John! John!*
and I was back again, in sunlight, hearing pitched
ongoing vibration of the one word: God; with the discordant

*

note: man, the un-
merciful; and the old song we all sing: God
is. And we
are not.

Report from a Far Place

for Fred Marchant

Sometimes, in impossible places, it is the small
illimitable pieces of the earth that will seduce you
back into grace: yellow sorrel in the hidden fissures,
the wren, spunk-tailed and pirouetting on the wood-pile,

splinters in the hewn timber you will relish
as imperfections. An orchid grows through wild grasses
the way the poem swells and will say *me!* this
being the first day again of all the world. You will be

witness to what a life saves out of the assault,
to prayers the defeated have no breath left to speak,
you will know the old, uncomplicated words

lifting once more like light, like love, like hope –
and you will find, at last, how the world writes itself
differently from what you had expected.

The Red Gate

Mornings, when you swing open the red gate –
admitting the world again with its creeds and wars –
the hinges sing their three sharp notes of protest;
you hear the poplars in their murmurings and sifflings
while the labouring high caravans of the rain
pass slowly by; it will seem as if the old
certainties of the moon and stars, mingled
with the turnings and returnings of your dreams, mist
to unreality, although there rise about you
matins and lauds of the meadow-sweet and rowan; the first
truck goes ruttling down the wet road and the raw
arguments, the self-betrayed economies of governments
assault you so you may miss the clear-souled drops
on the topmost bar that would whisper you peace.

The Chaplet

I can go back, quiet as a ghost, from here
where sweet coals whisper in the grate, I can go back –
while hailstones sputter against the panes outside – to see her
standing in the doorway, snow falling softly, an old woman's
spotted apron holding her, and know that she
is watching too, ghosting inwards and going back, visiting
her losses, as if she could find a way
to string it all together, to a sentence, making
sense, and I can sit remembering –
and shaping, the way a sonnet shapes –
that dusk her rosary burst asunder and beads
spilled skittering all-which-ways on the stone floor
as if her prayers and aspirations left
nothing in her shaking hands but a thread, bereft.

from A Little Book of Hours
(2008)

To Market, to Market

The day was drawky, with a drawling mist
coming chill across the marshlands;
the church of Ireland stood, damp and dumpy,
crows squabbling on its crenulated stump; cattle,

that had summered in a clover field, have been herded
through plosh and muck into a lorry, have dropped
their dung of terror on slat and road. Big
heavy-skulled heads, bellowing, stretch up

over the concrete wall for one clear glimpse
of the brown fields; and what of unredeemed
suffering? What of faithfulness? Spring
they were calling out of frustrated love

for their calves, how they stood in fields,
innocent and willing, uneasy in weighted flesh
like great-aunts whose trembling long-boned hands
fumble for something in old unstitching bags.

Call Me Beautiful

Broad-shouldered, big as a labouring man, Ruth
was egg-woman, slow and inarticulate,
flat-footed in her widowhood and her big sons

slap-witted, dun as she. I was ever dumb
before her, decades of harsh news
in the lines of her face, and a small smile

grateful for neighbourly busyness; each egg,
mucous-touched, she spat on and frotted clean
against black woollen skirts. Crucifix

over the door, painted Madonna on the sill,
her house was an island on chicken-shitted ground
with a harvesting of rushes, her world

not ordered by methodical thinking. Now I know
it is my own need disturbs me, to find
meaning and motive beyond the manifest

ungainliness, to seek the spirit's dance towards
divine friendship, and to vision her rapt
on her knees in a field of corn, gleaning.

Towards a Conversion

There is a soft drowse on the bog today;
the slight bog-cotton scarcely stirs; for now
this could be what there is of universe, the far-off
murmuring of ocean, the rarest traffic passing, barely

audible beyond the hill. I am all attention, held
like a butterfly in sunlight, achieve, a while,
an orchid quiet, the tiny shivering of petals, the mere
energy of being. Along the cuttings

bubbles lift through black water and escape, softly,
into sunlight; this complex knotting of roots has been
an origin, and nothing new nor startling
will happen here, save the growth of sphagnum

into peat; if this is prayer, then
I have prayed. I walk over millennia, the Irish
wolf and bear, the elk and other
miracles; everywhere bog-oak roots

and ling, forever in their gentle
torsion, with all this floor a living thing, held
in the world's care, indifferent. Over everything
voraciously, the crow, a monkish body hooded

in grey, crawks its blacksod, cleansing music;
lay your flesh down here you will become
carrion-compost, sustenance for the ravening roots;
where God is, has been, and will ever be.

Harbour: Achill Island

The winds come rushing down the narrow sound
between islands; from the north the whole
ocean pours through, exploding against boulders,
against landfalls, and courses into quiet
when the tide brims. A seal
lifts its grey-wise head out of the current, a mackerel
shoal sets the surface sparkling as it
passes. After the storm, light across the harbour
is a denser grey, soft-tinged with green; the whip
suddenness of lightning has shone this stolid
stonework fragile for an instant and the downpour
is a chariot drawn by six roan horses
pounding in across the sea. To the eye the water's
stilled now in the bay; stones on the sea-bed
shimmer like opals, cantankerous crustaceans
side-legging across the sand. I stand
awed again that this could be the still
point of all creation, the fruits
of a crazy generosity, yet how we amble through it
as if it were our portion, and our endeavour.

Mapping the Sky

These sharp nights you might see them – lines
etched in silver pencil between the stars, wide
family tree with names and dates and histories –
or skeletons in a dance so fast you scarcely
notice movement – a child's mobile where she lies
on her back in the cot, fingers and toes in an ecstasy
of mimicry. I, too, would dance if I could riddle
flesh sufficiently to find the source, make
feathers of my bones, to be with the clean birds
circling, and murderous. Now I must step indoors
from the cold to listen to the winds swing
caustic down the chimney, while the old and wise
pray for sailors out tonight on the wild seas,
for right balancing, for knowledge of the one star.

from A LITTLE BOOK OF HOURS (2008)

The Poem of the Goldfinch

Write, came the persistent whisperings, a poem
on the mendacities of war. So I found shade
under the humming eucalyptus, and sat,
patienting. Thistle-seeds blew about on a soft breeze,
a brown-gold butterfly was shivering on a fallen
ripe-flesh plum. Write your dream, said Love, of the total
abolition of war. Vivaldi, I wrote, the four
seasons. Silence, a while, save for the goldfinch
swittering in the higher branches, *sweet*, they sounded,
sweet-wit, wit-wit, wit-sweet. I breathed
scarcely, listening. Love bade me write but my hand
held over the paper; tell them you, I said,
they will not hear me. A goldfinch swooped,
sifting for seeds; I revelled in its colouring, such
scarlets and yellows, such tawny, a patterning
the creator himself must have envisioned, doodling
that gold-flash and Hopkins-feathered loveliness. Please
write, Love said, though less insistently. Spirit, I answered,
that moved out once on chaos… No, said Love,
and I said Michelangelo, Van Gogh. No, write
for them the poem of the goldfinch and the whole
earth singing, so I set myself down to the task.

Kane's Lane

The substance of the being of Jesus
sifts through the substance of mine; I
am God, and son of God, and man. Times I feel

my very bones become so light I may
lift unnoticed above Woods's Wood and soar
in an ecstasy of being over Acres' Lake; times again

I am so dugged, so dragged, my flesh
falls granite while a fluid near congealed
settles on my heart. The Christ – frozen in flight

on the high-flung frame of his cross –
leaves me raddled in the grossest of mercies
and I walk the length of Kane's Lane, on that ridge

of grass and cress and plantain
battening down the centre, I sex my tongue
on the flesh juices of blackberries, cinch my jaws on the chalk

bitterness of sloes, certain and unsettled,
lost and found in my body, sifted through a strait
and serpentine love-lane stretched between dawn and night.

Stranger

I too have gone down into my underworld
    seeking my father, as he went down into his;
we go on believing there is the possibility
    of discovering the rich knowledge that is held

like a life in amber and that we can return
    certain of what business we should be about. Here
is the very edge of dream, this the marsh, a green miasma
    hovering above; small birds, motionless, cling

to the reeds, like terror-stricken souls. You must cross
    in your journey, broad rivers spanned
by magnificent structures; you must cross, too,
    the laboured hills of Aquitaine and the neat

villages of Picardy. Great trucks go rushing by
    to somewhere that will not concern you; you pass
cherry trees by the roadside with their blood
    fruits, leave behind you

château, auberge, the diminished whisperings
    of wars; you will pass, too, fields of sunflowers,
those astonished and childish faces lifted
    in congregation. At a great distance the rough-cast

white of the highest mountains will appear at evening
    tipped with baby-pink; folk-art in medieval hill-top chapels
will draw out tears of innocence; in the baroque theatricals
    of later overwhelming churches, ghastly saints

will be sitting in their skeletal remains, grinning from glass caskets
    like dowdy stuffed birds; they shall remain for ever silent
and joyful on their couches. When you emerge, shaken, and carrying
    the ever-heavier burden of yourself, you may seek

solace in words, for the world burns to know what news
 the deepest darkness holds, but oh how you find
the words themselves pallid and languorous, so shy
 they lurk in hidden places like the most secretive

night animals. You will survive, you know, only as long
 as you hold to the narrow footpath, speaking your father's name
as if it served as talisman and wondering, when their time comes,
 will your children too go down into their underworld, seeking.

Madonna and Child

in memoriam, Mary Josephine Deane, née Connors

8th December; the day dawns dark, a slow
rain drawling across the suburbs; one bedraggled dog
chaws at something out of a spilled bin; wind-tortured leaves
blow wet against a litter-spattered wall.
News on the radio, wars, aggression, the old
indomitable hatreds; 'Lord,' she would quote,
'you are hard on mothers…'

A graceless urbscape, with arrogant magpies
clacking at indifferent cats, and only
a winter-flowering cherry spilling blossoms
over the garden wall. Fumes from the car
hanging on thick air, I reverse onto Cypress Downs,
mother on my mind, decades of guilt and dole, and no
way through to her, no way through to me. 8th

December, I hear it again, that scream of pain
forced from a proud woman; a midwife
(eager for fags and a rutted lane towards home)
stepping on stone-tiled floors with a tsk-tsk sharpness,
holds basin, linen, the instruments of her art. Such
an inconceivable moment, and I am intimately
involved. Grey day, and cold, with the fire
of a suffering beyond my comprehension. For which,
mother, these thanks, these
decades late, these my pleas
for your forgiveness. Irish Catholic mother, fortress
besieged, Tower of Ivory, House of Gold…

December 8th, and feast-day, the word immaculate
driving her, too, from my comprehension
and my love. A dark morning, grey daylight, this winter

softened by advent calendars and cards, people
congregate at shopping centres, how many days
to Christmas? At the start of every journey, gather
nourishment, the *Irish Times*, bars of chocolate, three
perfect pink hyacinths in a white ceramic pot.

*

We were heading south, towards the low hills; Ursula
reading aloud this morning's office, the psalms,
the antiphons and aspirations.
The road above the city had a winter clarity,
the Wicklow hills redeeming
field, hedgerow and pasture; trees standing,
a spray of mud coating their trunks,
for this is quarry road,
                              with trucks
hauling away the innards from the lumpen hills, pressing
muck into the tarmac, a misting of muck
everywhere; from branches of a diseased elm a crow,
in black cassock, grey soutane, was preaching
though in high dudgeon, to the world.
                                    If it was father
who came out with me into the winter night,
who climbed the quarry hill to watch the stars, an icy
breathing of island darkness holding us about
yet it was she, perhaps, was held indoors
by indoor things, oven concerns, and bucket suds;
son to father, cherishing, to mother
distant and different, in a dim and dimming otherness.

                              Over a clutch of dung
a whorl of dancing flies turns in regulated chaos
like a universe of stars. Movement of hard-hat men –
Homeric statement of yellow overalls, of warrior
boots – the revving-up of trucks, inexorable

from A LITTLE BOOK OF HOURS (2008)

whittling at the core of earth for the next
crude gobbets of wealth. Big
men, big-chested, certain of what they are about.

*

Madonna. Miriam. Mary. There are those more beautiful
who pass like caravans on a near horizon
laden with gold out of Egypt and Ophir; she
snub-nosed, brown-skinned and undernourished, wears a few
beads of coloured glass, speaks unlovely dialect;
there are homes more beautiful, porticoes
for the moderately-off, and mansion keeps
of granite stone and marble step, cool chambers; hers

a mud-brick two-roomed shape, crowded
with family, and the lower spaces shelter sheep; hers
a brushwood roof where she can sleep at night
under the silent tumultuous stars;
she weaves, prepares and grinds, she herds,
she is a drudge, hands callused and body sore;
without dowry, scarce past puberty,
and who should desire her, save the God?

*

The first town, Blessington, long street with new streets off
into neat and manifold estates. Grey forenoon,
pre-Christmas busyness, bulbs hung above the street
and wavering in the slightest breeze; commerce,
a focusing on Santa-lit big windows, banks
festooned with winter sleighs and much-loved reindeer,
people hurrying, wrapped about themselves, hasty
bonhomie and compliments of the season. We drive
through, watchful, pausing from the breathing of the psalms.

She would sit at the kitchen table,
copies piled on the parti-coloured frayed oil-cloth,
grandfather bustling in from sheds, and father
pacing the floor like a displaced animal; she would tell
over and over the pounds and shillings and pence,
tut at the spellings, and the dull
reiteration of the island girls' ordinary days,
                                        their lot
housewifery or service, the slow labouring into flesh
laden with black wools and waitingness, or their lot
exile, housewifery or service, their arms akimbo over full
breasts, hurrying into memories, nostalgia, waitingness…
and she loved them, their staring eyes, the wool
socks inside black boots, the patchwork skirts
and cardigans, and would hymn a strict
heaven before them, a catechism of purity and care,
with tiny versicles of miracle, the sun
glancing off mauve hillside heathers onto the painted
classroom walls – till she sat back at the table, and sighed,
the pencil paused from its ticking, light fading.
                                        Something
hydrangea-like about her, mop-head, lace-cap,
how it flourished with extravagance under a kindly sun
and hung its head all brown and frowsty against the soils
of winter; if you plant nails in the earthed roots
the lace-caps alter colour; and she hoarded
sorrow at her base till it grew a virtue in her, weaponry
to hurl sorrows back against a wounding world;
Madonna. Mother. Mary Jo.

                              *

She is not dressed in satins, nor sitting idle at a prie-dieu;
the messenger, when he comes, comes
like a fox, magister of the subtlest arts
of being. Miriam was small, robust and muscular,

she sat in the dooryard, plucking chickens, the smaller
feathers irritating fingers, her smock
spattered with blood after the killing; from the far
end of the yard a goat's laughter and nearer
the pharaoh strutting of a cock; but her dark eyes
watched beyond the hen-shit; if she could not read
nor write, she held the history of the tribes
vividly in memory, could see past the blood
               of Nahum, Samson, Abel
into the hurt and tender eyes of God; hers
an unremarkable graced dailiness, though why the Spirit
should fall on her out of the chaos she did not
understand, she did not understand.

*

Driving between low humped hills, a curved
valley and, on the right, the small and laggard stream
that will become the Slaney. Father's eager stalking
of the river's pools, how a man cleaves
to a woman, she to him, down all the bright
dark days of their togetherness. And I tune to the radio –
Vivaldi, the music such sweet bitterness,
              nulla in mundo pax sincera.
I watched her in the big bedroom, Achill, she sat
before the dressing-table, her favourite
tortoiseshell-framed hand-mirror before her face;
it was something in the stillness moved me, I saw
she was watching far beyond, out the big window
across bogland towards the distant sound,
unmoving, though her lifted hand was trembling slightly;
how the souls of those who have passed come smiling
across an inner vision that strikes us numb, at times,
though restless: witnesses, to assoil the living, on the trail
the dead have passed along, and cautioning. She shivered,
suddenly, laughed towards me and said: I think
somebody has walked across my grave.

After one day's mongering and dole he stands
to ponder the life of a man, a Jew-boy, this day's
exorbitant samenesses, all the days like peels
of white wood curling in the corner of a yard;
where a stream flows down from the snow mountain
into the lake, the woman, Jew-girl, scarce past puberty,
has spread linens out over scorched grass, stands
in the shade of a tree, dreaming: of a Jew-boy, a house;
she turns, there in the gentle emptiness of the day,
laying her tunic down, moving her dark-brown body gratefully
into the lake; beautiful the movements, her hands
piling the grape-black hair at her nape, bone of her spine
enchanting as she wades in water till she stands,
waves lapping her breasts, the rose evening
breathlessly still, as he is, watching.

She turns and her small breasts are firm
in the fading light, the flower of her navel,
the darkening delta of her maidenhair and her thighs
rising out of the water, the water
tiny golden gifts against her skin;
she stands, unabashed, a while, her hands
gentle against the stomach-flesh, and he stands,
watching; she dresses, still wet, lightened
by her bathing and he hears her voice, a soft
and animal laughter as she moves along the shore
to stand in quiet praise and be a part of it,
the dark of early night, the trees, the water.
Out in the yard tonight they will tell
tall stories, they will sing sad songs
to the night-birds, to the kindly stars; he
will be silent, hushed in himself, and wondering.

*

She is sitting on a rug, hugging herself small
inside the wind; she is beyond the fray
of family.
                    Offshore the waves
swell impetuously and break
as a line of foam goes racing angularly
across the crests, the break and long-flow reaching in
along the beach. She has been reading
a murder mystery, but something – voice or gull
or sudden catch of sorrow – has her pause, and hold
the book against her breast to watch
inwards; the beauty, the enormity of the Atlantic
won't touch her there; her ganglion of nerves,
of bone and flesh and tissue holds a moment
out of the impetus as she penetrates, despite herself,
the dreadful wall that lifts always
against our littleness. I see her shudder, her eyes
recover the wild light of sea and she returns,
gratefully, to the artificial mystery.

*

As an orchid among buttercups is she, as a peach tree
among brambles in the wood; as exile
in a hostile land, as drudge among the very poor.
Sometimes the soul, swollen with the news of creation,
grows too great for the body and leads it forth
on a journey, over fruitless hillsides, across stone-ridden
uplands, in an outflow of praise and wonder. Hers, yet,
a long apprenticeship to pain, before she grows
mistress of it, and settles down to the long night.

*

Left at the filling station; you've been down this road…
Mine is a raid on memory, the needed booty –
forgiveness; how we misunderstand each other,
willfully sometimes, more usually
out of ignorance and conceit.
                           Suddenly a rabbit, colour
of milked tea but with white ankle-socks and a Christ-child
scut of the purest white; a nibbler, big-bidder,
delicate on the scutch-tips, and wary. We passed
the wayside grotto, Madonna, lime-white and blue-gloss,
having little to do with our passing, this stylised
bathetic woman, not mother, a place
to burn small lights, ushering prayers away
in streels of smoke. These lowroads, twisting
to the ancient laying-out of fields, dull, untaxing.

                       *

She moved, unnoticed, among many
in the caravanserai, road-weary, wearied too
by the not-to-be-admitted knowledge; slept
with the animals, their warmth, their comfortable
snores and shufflings in the dark;
the camel drivers were speaking quietly together
the world's gossip, and how the tetrarch
was building palaces to himself; the muleteers
in the other yard talked drunkenly, farted, argued;
games of dice, the stench of sweat and greed;
until she slipped away, beyond the dawn, into
cinnamon-coloured hills, a merlin
circling round its cry and tiny furred and frightened lives
busy amongst the rocks and scrub. The world
                    troubled, and everywhere the powerful
fattening on detritus of rioting and wars. And sat, stilled,
small and invisible on a parched slope, in need
of woman-talk and sustenance, scared of the journey done,
more scared of the journey yet to come.

from A LITTLE BOOK OF HOURS (2008)

Here is a man whose dreams bear fruit. And here
is Nazareth, a village without importance, and Aramaic,
a language of strange utterance; here is Miriam, betrothed,
a girl of no importance, poor, unlearned, menial, drudge.
Here is a man, Torah-observing Jew, big-handed,
scarcely-worded carpenter, and the angels visit him
in his dreams. In cases like these, they tell us, marriage
comes first and love, perhaps, comes later.

      My soul extols the greatness of the Lord
and my spirit exults in God who saves me,
for he has heeded and loved the lowliness of his servant.
And see, from this day out every generation shall know me blest,
for the mightiest One has worked wonderful things for me
                      and holy is his name.
Down all the generations his mercy swells to those who love him.
And in this way the strength of God has been made manifest:
the arrogant in the hardness of their heart have been strewn about,
and the powerful pulled from their thrones, our God
has lifted up on high those who had been degraded;
he has fed the hungry full with the best of gifts
and those who are rich have been banished empty from his sight.
Remembering the greatness of his mercy
he has come to the aid of the oppressed,
for this has been his promise from the distant past
and will be kept down all the centuries to come.

                      *

I was sent in with messages; there was a hum
from the two-roomed schoolhouse, her
fiefdom; without democracy, for its own good;
here she stood, mistress, the word 'mother'
would not apply. In the small hallway
there was a smell of cocoa and damp coats;
for me the embarrassment of girls, their smirks,

their implausible and whispered comments.
A sudden silence as I moved across to her desk,
chalk-marks on the blackboard, the whole puzzle
being elucidated in one of its smaller parts;
and now? after decades: the school become
a woodwork shop, become, after failure, an abandoned
husk, small dunes of wood-dust, shavings, something
banging in the breeze with mild-mannered impatience,
and only persistent island winds that come fingering
grass and nettle, rust-work, and love, long missed.

*

They had gone on beyond the city, her pains
causing her to cry out at times and he, hurt
and ignorant and distraught, led the reluctant ass
towards the shelter of hills; a low, blue-black sky,
stars sharp already as nails, a chill wind blowing;
he would lay her down among the scrub, if necessary,
the donkey-blanket beneath her, water from a stream
to help the cleansing; there would be night-birds,
jackals, perhaps, and snakes. The great howl of the ass
frightened him and he held the woman tightly
against the cruelties of shale and the unshareable pangs
of a full pregnancy. Till the gathering dark
drew them to a small fire; in the limestone hills
a cave, small shelter against the winds, and crude
half-drunk shepherds gobbing at a fire; they heard
small life-sounds, the shiftings of a flock
and she cried again, as the lost do, against the pain.

*

Out once more on the main road, Carlow / Enniscorthy;
I eased my grip on the wheel; a truck

sent up a spray of dirtied rain as I sped past;
I remember thinking how much I love the woman
quiet beside me on this searing trip. Mount Leinster
invisible in the gathered mists, this rich-soil land
fallow and puddled in the Irish winter. Slaney
broader now, its dark flow soiled with a factory's
olive outspill, and trees being hacked out of the way
for some no-doubt necessary building. I reached,
touching the woman's hand, for presence, reassurance, warmth.

*

Walnuts, figs; the tiniest hairs of the gooseberry;
she would touch the sap of balsam trees
to her children's skin, cure headache and weeping eyes;
she would rub docken leaves where the sting of nettles
scalded. Morning, the jacaranda tree letting go
its misty dreaming, it could be again the outset of the world
where man and animal stand astonished; under the dreeping bush
she sets out, deep-breathing, to take her place before the class;
her children brought to task, the strange one
hungry at the carpenter's desk; there is poverty, taxation, a little
beggary, and at times her own unruly sons
pestering the neighbours; she prepares a barley porridge,
for supper there will be cucumbers, onions, nuts and oranges;
on each fourth Sabbath, with luck, a salted fish; potato bread and farl,
cabbage cooked in bacon stock, thick and smoked rasher slices;
on Fridays herring, in Lent one meal and two collations.

*

And then we were slowing down the long hill
into Bunclody; a varied shrubbery, the small town
laying itself out below; a soft-toned town, to retire to.

I ease the car to a halt, opposite the bungalow, memories
like exhaust fumes stirring through the heavy air; there
the plants he nursed, soil he laboured; that window
was her room, her privacy, her prayer-time, ministries;
blank now, reflecting this bleak day, and unresponding.
After her death, the house loud with visitors, I slept
alone in her room and in her bed; the moon sent a dull,
pre-Christmas light through the curtains; I knew, at last,
a weight of sadness, a slow welling of loss; a scent
remained, her talcs and creams, the dressing-table things,
a glass tea-tray for rings and hairpins, and there
in the empty hours after dawn, I saw
her tortoiseshell hand-mirror, dusted,
and a crinkled prayer-card to Saint Anthony, patron
of all lost things. Mother. Who has taken away with her
her bundles of sufferings, inflated anxieties
for her children's souls, and every possibility
of mutual understanding and forgiveness.
                                            On then,
the river again on our left, through the rich and fallow fields
till we drew up, at last, by the graveyard wall
under dripping trees. That certain pause, a small
silence, and then the gathering of coats, umbrellas,
the pot with its three pink hyacinths. The car doors
closed, startling through the almost stillness of the rain,
intrusive ping-song of the automatic lock, and then,
destination, the rising recurrent sorrow of the merely
human before loss, its unacceptability, its disdain.

*

8th December. 1943.
The world was stretched
feverish under war. There was a fall
of snow, they told me, over the heathlands.
Achill. My island. Call me

John. After the Evangelist. And Francis, after the poor
and love-tossed fool. And call me
Mary, for the day that's in it, and for mother, worn
after the pain and tearing. There were men
wading through an underworld of blood and muck
uncomprehending. I hear the winter storms
crying through the pine grove. Mother. Mary.
Mother and son. Madonna. A winter child.

*

After it all, after all this, the years, the distances,
after the days and absences and angers, what can I do
but stand in stillness by the grave, her name
and his, only a dream breeze touching
the trees and a soft rain falling? Stand,
nothing to say, all said, winter, and grey,
my presence I hope amounting to something,
to sorrow, pleading, the three pink hyacinths.
I step across her grave to lay them by the headstone,
offering a presence more eloquent than mine.
        Mother again, and child,
the light along the body is olive green; I wonder
if they would have draped him across her knees? The blood,
the gore, the fluids. I wonder if she even had
that much comfort? This loved and cared-for body
torn now, reviled; that she bore and birthed
in anxiety and sorrow; God's abandonment of him
is doubly hers. And can you hear them all, the women?
Mothers, daughters, sisters... their cries
across time and space, joining with her in ongoing silence
that shatters the world across every century,
crying against war and killing, against crucifixion, torture, rape,
the fact of the disappeared, the pulling down of love.

NEW AND SELECTED POEMS

Triduum

I had been reading Dante and was shaken once again
how we suffer appalling punishment for being human;
I stepped out to breathe awhile in the good air.

After yesterday's excess this sacred Saturday was still;
adult hares played in the wild meadow; across the hedgerow
ash and larch broke against the skyline, but all I saw was the Christ

with his contained sufferings, stride down the laneways of Sheol
calling aloud redemption. I almost stepped on a baby hare
crouched low and coloured as the dun rushes, dying, it seemed,

the eyes glazed over. It was a long day, sluggish with vague
expectations, and the long night dark and untenanted. Morning,
when I carried out the ashes, finch and wren and robin

washed the hedgerows with a rioting of song; and suddenly
the baby hare! Insolent, nibbling the edges of new growth
on the fern till I clapped my hands, impatient against such

disturbance, and it glanced at me, and slowly loped away.

from Eye of the Hare
(2011)

Travelling Man

I was sitting in the waiting lounge, watching out onto the apron.
There were, as usual, works,
men in hard hats, yellow orange blue, with trucks and JCBs and such

chaos everywhere you would wonder if there could be
anyone in charge.
An Exxon Mobil aviation-fuel truck went by;

I heard its thundering through the thick-glass window,
felt the floor
shuddering and I thought

of the earthedness of islands, of grandmother kneading dough
for her apple and blackberry tart,
a small flouring through the hairs on her arms. Thought, too,

of the island crossroads on a Fair day, loud voices greeting,
animals skittering, the agreeable
racketing of hooves and cart-wheels across the tarred road;

left, to Keel, right to Achill Sound, long silences between passings,
and the sea, in the near distance, sounding.
Here, in Heathrow, Terminal 2, an organised confusion, an all-ways

drift and hurrying, chattering, baby-cries; alarming
head-shapes and body-forms,
children calling out in babelish grunts and noises;

left, to Athens, Düsseldorf, Algiers, right
to Munich, Sibiu and – later – home.
Then I was thirty thousand feet above the fields and towns of
                                                                          Europe,

on a pitted and upflung untarred highway of air, the craft
pitched to left, to right,
like the twig I floated down the drain after a heavy

summer shower, and I thought once more of the hold,
the bold solidity, of islands
for how can you forget the sea

sounding perpetually within you, its lift
and fall, its lift
and fall, for I have come from far from such earthedness

where you may go down through layer and layer of man-bone,
of fish-bone, fish-clay, shale and scale,
from the washed-out dust of mountains, down to original molluscs

and the shaking fingers of the God.

Shelf Life

From a side-hook in the pantry, *Old Moore's*
Almanac for 1943, its pages browned from the pipe-smoke
of Grandpa Time, and one china cup without its handles,
a small blue boat drifting towards the bridge; one

Knock-shrine mug, repository for two brass keys
that have lost their locks; a brawn-coloured oval
roasting-dish, its cracked-over surface criss-crossed
with the trackways of old Europe; a Rowntree's Cocoa tin,

its comely maiden watching out onto hurrying time
with a face of wonder; a carriage clock without its hands,
standing in its final after-tock; Hallowe'en tin rings
without their lustre; a Brigid's Cross, the rushes dried

brittle as old wicks; and there, in a cardboard box,
the mixed-up bits of Lego, Meccano, jigsaws, those
building blocks of a world to be. Two off-green, birthday
balloons, wrinkled and out-of-breath, string still knotted

like scarves on their scrawny necks, and there, on the top shelf
my tinware porringer from lunchtime school, long emptied
of my peaceful indifference to all things. Finally, me, here
mooching about in my ghosthood over shelves no longer there.

The Marble Rail

I came up against the marble rail, carrying
a weight of Latin and other mysteries: men
on the left side, women on the right. I got down
to studying heads of horses on the women's scarves,
how big men knelt, one knee down on cap or hanky,
left hand to the jaw, eyes loose, fingers twitching.
There was acknowledged presence of a people's God,
snuffling, reticent, unwilling and cajoled;
I took the strange moon-bread they fed me
and turned a half a century down the aisle
to where I still attend, waiting among a frail
seniority of old Ireland, and the blood of the God
has the savour of vintage sherry and His flesh
is a melting of ashes across the tongue.

On the Edge

in memoriam Gerry O'Malley

In retrospect
there was a tenderness to the day,
a delicacy in the midst of dread;

in the year's completion –
hydrangeas soggy brown, the plum tree branches
black and brittle – there were yet

clusters of snowdrops
as in the blest beginnings while the wind
spirited signatures across the rancid grasses

and playfully
erased them. The winter day
stretched clean and bright, the coffin came to rest on spars

over the deep-dug grave
like a new ship waiting to be launched.
In retrospect

there was a homeliness to the field
in its cold purity, while a train went by
beyond the trees and a plane rose, shimmering,

into the bluest sky.
We were holding on to the last prayers,
to the better memories, to the harmonies of wreathe

and bouquet; I thought
of last night's waking, only his face
visible above the lace and silk, like a mild

Quixote
or a Frans Hals *grand seigneur*. Now we were
holding on, the gravediggers waiting patiently

nearby. Then
he was lowered, the wilful rites
completed, we, with the brute and idling earthedness

standing numb, complicit
in the necessity of things. A flight of wood doves
passed like an exhalation over our heads, the wings

applauding loudly;
and there was order everywhere. In retrospect
there was something beautiful to the day. And unacceptable.

Eye of the Hare

There! amongst lean-to grasses and trailing vetch
catch her? – vagrant, free-range and alert;

I saw the eager watch-tower of the ears, I knew
the power of legs that would fling her into flight;

concentrate, he said, and focus: you must love
the soft-flesh shoulder-muscles where the bullet bites,

caress – and do not jerk – the trigger: be all-embracing, be
delicate. I had no difficulty with the saucepan lid

down at the end of the meadow, lifted, for practice,
against the rhododendron hedge, I could sight

its smug self-satisfaction and shoot a hole
pea-perfect and clean through. Attention to the hare

left me perplexed for I, too, relish the vision
I imaged in its round dark eye, of a green world

easy under sunlight, of sweet sorrel and sacred herbs –
and I turned away, embarrassed, and absolved.

from EYE OF THE HARE (2011)

Cedar

In what year of war did Jehovah
abandon them? A man
riding a Yamaha XS 400 model 1982
has taken his two daughters from the ruins of their house,
has left the battered bodies of his wife and mother
among the rubble and tries to flee
across the baked, beloved fields of Lebanon –
into a hole somewhere, please God, the two
children, terrified, big eyes filled with tears, fingers
gripping hard but the bike will scarcely move, it sputters, skids,
one child before him, one behind, both tied to him
with light-blue clothes-line round their waists, the bike
slithers out into the day and turns, please
God, north on a cratered road, the sky itself so beautiful, such
an immaculate creation, and the children's voices wail
louder than the stop-go reluctant coughing of the bike
till an Israeli F16, inaudible, well-nigh invisible, so high
above, oh God please God, draws
a gash of fumes across the sky
and father, daughters, bike explode into shards
of flesh and chrome and are lost
in the bleak inheritance of the Old Testament
while only the back wheel of the bike
a Yamaha XS 400 model 1982
spins in uproarious speed and will
not stop, will not
stop

Abundance

Over the surface of the hillside,
its crannies, its low-slung water gullies,
there is a lemon-yellow glow, like light, like pollen-flush;

you and I
have breathed together such abundance
as if it were the music of a slow, profound love song,

have stood side by side, calmed
by the sheltering dimness within a stand of pines.
Once I climbed, letting my fingertips poach on pine bark and take

the teardrops to themselves, and grow
sticky with the life-sorrow of tree. This, too,
abundance. Remember those ordinary men – heavy-fleshed

and leather-handed –
who were taken out of ordinary day
and heisted into the texture of the wonderful,

wishing there would never be an outcome:
James, Peter, John… yet how they missed
the caulking of heavy-keeled boats, the gutting of fish;

they, and all of us (ah, my dear)
will stride into the welcoming arms of mercy
that day we soar off grandpa earth to take a place, living,

among starlight. The word *shrive*
touches on it, the way old grumpy Abraham
hauled himself on high along the rough-hemp rope of his faith.

The Colours

These the colours of the seasons: gold
for the portal flowering of birth; violet

for shy kisses in a shaded copse, for days
of fast and pleading, for the iris of Van Gogh;

rose, for one long day of joy, for the survival
of sea-thrift on a famished cliff-face ledge;

suburban avenues will be clothed
in the alb of cherry-blossom white;

white and gold the chasuble
of the chestnut tree, and white

for angels flying in to the festival of snow, for virgins
crossing all together the frozen ice-paths of the Alps;

red, for martyrs, for the late-year standing of the dogwood,
the gift of tongues, the long delay of Good Friday

and the blood-stained building blocks of Gaza;
green, for the ordinary days, *de tempore* labouring,

for past time, in-between times and times ahead of times;
gold again, for the mind's embossed

portal to the sacrament, and black
for the peaceful, the having-come-through, dead.

The Colliery

They closed the colliery, putting full-stop
to a dark page. They had gone down into black earth
in search of light and warmth, ingesting cold

and clothed in darkness. Their slender picks
were fashioned like those delicately nibbed pens
with which we scratched our first letters onto slates,

C for cat, for coal. On their foreheads, fixed, a third eye.
Aeneas, Dante, Hercules, went down anticipating
certain return but these, like Orpheus, found themselves

doubtful of success; here was no option for caprice
nor the exercise of pure reason; to survive
was to become like matter, so to lift again towards light.

They planted dynamite, like seeds, the mountain
rumbling in sudden pain, and some apologised each time,
for being human. Now they are learning words again,

names for stars in the black sky, for blue on the sloe's skin,
for rust on the swallow's throat. Wondering, as I do,
if anything in the world will ever wash us clean.

Words of the Unknown Soldier

He stumped us, this Jesus of yours, with his
walking on water, fandango, entrechat, glissade;
birthing, imagine! in a dark cave, out of all knowing; then

he walked the hard-baked earth of Palestine, but not
as you walk, or as I, for behind him the healing flowers grew,
the rosebay willowherb, chamomile, the John's wort;

we noted, too, that he could walk through walls,
appearing suddenly in the midst of folk as if
he were always there, waiting that they might notice him;

oh yes, this too, he walked on air
leaving them gawping upwards as he rose
higher and higher, like a skylark, walking

into the invisible. That was later. But humankind
will not be cheated of its prey for we claimed him,
hailing him fast to a tree, that he could not move

on water, earth or air, and we buried him in the underearth.
Where, it is said, he took to walking once again,
singing his larksong to the startled, to the stumped, dead.

Shoemaker

He sat, cross-legged, on a deal table
as if dropped, ready-made, from an old myth;
sat, all hours, all days, lips pursed and fingers
deft and fast, like the poet

who could see the world through a needle's eye,
difficult though penetrable, a shifting, leathery mass
that might be shaped to something
beautiful, and lasting. Like the itinerant Christ

walking the ranges of Galilee, nowhere to lay down
his head. When I conjugate
Christ, and longing, what I mean
is the lake behind the cobbler's house, its waters

soothing us constantly across the night;
I mean trees, those summer mornings,
standing high and stilled within their being; on wilder days
the winds make shapes amongst them,

ghosts visiting the house, composing
their wind-leaf harmonies: I want to be able to say, again,
Christ. Our island shoemaker
sat, sometimes, outside, half-concentrating, half-

watching people go the road; he was one
in a guild with swallows and the blooming of the haw,
one with the people who went measuring their steps
in to the small chapel to divine their living, who watched

snow falling, visible through the stained glass windows, flakes
that could be birds migrating, butterflies, or spirits
out on spirit escapades. When I write
cobbler, last or nail, or when I scribble

wine, or bread, or music, what I am stitching for
is Christ, is how love still may permeate
the rush of trucks along the motorways, spray
rising against the windscreens, the wipers sighing.

Sheets

When she was through with them, the sheets
roistered on a sunbright day in off-the-Atlantic breezes;
Nanna washed them, there at the lake's edge, the water
a golden brown from the heather-hillside's leeching;
she trampled them in the sandy shallows, scrubbed
with a hard red soap and trampled them again;
sometimes she sang – holding long skirts up
in both hands – an air of maiden Ireland in her pains;
she stretched them out over a rock, or floated them
over the clover-speckled grass in an easing sun;
noon-time, on the high line, they were yawls,
spinnakers or topsails, sometimes clapping loud
at unexpected liberties. When I slept between them
they were elemental arms, holding me in her love.

Bikes

At the crossroads a big, joint-squealing gate
leads from the back yard to the road, an opening
out from the known world. Neighbours came
to leave their high-framed dray-horse bikes
slouched to the wall inside the gate, and took the bus
to their destinations. We assumed free rein
and took to pedalling round the yard, the bikes
bucking like jittery donkeys at our hands. But oh
how we raced, wee riders, relishing all the while
a watchful guilt, a boldness always on the point
of tears at a gashed knee or a sideways fall
into a tangle of chain and handlebars. We earned
accumulated secrecies when the travellers returned
puzzled at fine-groomed bikes standing to attention.

Ever This Night

for Herbert Lomas

There was a rose-petal sky all evening
showing from clouds that were turf-shaped and dense;
a full moon lifted behind the pine-grove and four
whooper swans flew low towards the lake,
crying, you would think,
for the familiar wastes of Iceland. I tucked down
into the warmth of the big bed, rosary beads
still curled about my fingers. I thought
how the angel would guard me across the ocean floor
of the night – then wondered, what would my angel do
in her boredom, pent in her God-given cage
of air: be watchful lest I slip into some crevasse?
or step towards the maw of a leviathan, great white
or giant squid? I drifted, bemused
that an angel's bones might be coloured
moon-white, star-blue? Feathers colour-patterned
like a goldfinch? Sleep, then, like high tide settling,
I was carried away, sails billowing, to find myself
down amongst the old and harmless wrecks, great
grandfather Ted, great-uncle John. All through the night
I was island, wide spaces opening
off every degree of the compass, life before me, its scenes
already melting into air, into thin air;
and came awake next morning, safe, and dry,
colour-patterned seashells in my hands, like dreams.

Footfalls

It is April,
    dry and hot as summer;
        wisteria languishes
like an overdressed society dame
    at a chamber concert, and purple tulips
        speak of cemeteries and sex;
in Montparnasse
    tourists have a field day,
        avenues and alleyways laid out
as rationally as an old faubourg;
    the dead
        putting on a show,
the living
    sauntering by as if nothing mattered, not
        now, perhaps not ever. Here
is Brancusi's kiss,
    womanman embracing
        as if to cleave forever;
Sartre and de Beauvoir
    have nothing new to say
        though finely suited businessmen
pass by with cameras.
    Listen to that chuckling sound –
        Saint-Saëns at it again,
doodling notes that touch
    on the bones of sunshine,
        piccolo-runs like tickled trout
finning their way towards death.
    But we have come
        for Beckett,
to stand in numb and silent thanks
    that someone led us to the edge
        and did not push,
though he impelled himself beyond the limit
    and told us of it.
        No ego-surfeiting. No longer
waiting. Move
    softly by. Like leaf-fall. Like echo's bones.
        Samuel, *salut!*

Midsummer Poem

for Gerard Smyth

These are the grey nights, high tide, high summer.
Ash-trees in the hedgerows are stirring in the mists
and you can see the fields laid out in shifting patterns;

somewhere in the night a cow is lowing, sorrowful
as a distant foghorn; dreams are disturbed, something
gleams a moment and will disappear, like a sea trout

rising, like a distant phosphorescence; breezes
that come shuffling through the alders are the breathing
of waves against a strand; no need to fear

ghosts of your loved dead who go drifting by, offshore,
their dark sails holding; the Joseph lilies, the white
Canterbury bells, hold within them, as you do,

their own light and though they will sink through the rough
autumn days, as you will, they have worked wonders
and will resurface, firmer in themselves and more fruitful.

Mimizan Plage

I know the meaning of the words: *hosanna* and *halleluia*,
the shout, and the long-drawn-out quavering belly-note:

Betty, who could not dance, dancing for exuberance
on the scullery table and Gerry shouting *Dia leat!*

you, on the beach at Mimizan;

porpoises beyond the waves at Keel, in slow ballet
over and under the ocean, stitching the sea to sky;

and you, on the beach at Mimizan;

Róisín, not watching, Tim watching out
as the car climbed through mile-high Italian villages;

you, on the beach at Mimizan;

jasmine blossoms, like milk-stars brilliant
against a dark-green sky, scenting the suburbs;

and you, on the beach at Mimizan, the red wine warming,
salamis, olives, rolls, and our hearts thundering.

SNOW FALLING ON CHESTNUT HILL

Overture

Freude, Tochter aus Elysium

Joseph lilies sway, in choir, like a soft-throated chorus
of snow-coifed nuns; you stand, distant from them,
child of God, suffering God. On sodden fields

a flock of chittering starlings shifts; the eye
is never worn with seeing, nor the ear filled
with hearing. *Freude*, the poet wrote, *trinken alle Wesen*

an den Brüsten der Natur; all things
nourish themselves on joy at the breasts
of Nature. Here: the field, its wet-daub acres

ragged as a famine-smitten family, only the rushes
flourishing, their knot-rooted stubborn uselessness,
the matted shivering of scutch grasses, persistent

betrayal by the rains. Bitter
as the ribs of hounds: and yet
we hold within our hearts rich meadows

of the mercy of God, all of us –
forgiving and forgiven – riveted
by the outstretched arms of the Christ-man;

made light by sorrows, and by astonishment.
By the gold-flush blossoming of furze bushes
round the edges of the field. Swallows

are flying low over the wild meadow and already
summer symphonies are giving way
to organ-fugues of the fall; child of God,

suffering God, I have moved so many years
across uncertainties, listening for that slow
basso profundo, source and sustenance of grief, of joy...

Freude!

*

I think of that old cantankerous composer, deaf
as his podium, how he waved his hands about and heard
his *Ninth Symphony*'s shout of joy; and marvel how he stood
gazing out across the blurred and many

faces of death's company (full
orchestra, full chorus) who sang : *Brüder, überm Sternenzelt
Muss ein lieber Vater wohnen!* Brothers, above
the canopy of stars, a loving Father lives!

*

Father walked the kitchen floor
evenings, hands clenched behind his back;
mother held her head down, there had been disputes

and the air was dense
from withholding presences; she prayed
Legion of Mary prayers, whispered militancy, the sibilances

irritating. There sank within me,
down to irretrievable depths, the bellied sails
of pleading and the rusting anchor of guilt.

When mother had whispered her way into her heaven,
father sank into his depths, telling sins
on the ambit of his rosary,

bead after bead, a slow circuit.

Now, I, child of the times,
have been down to the shore again;
I hold his old brown chaplet,

crucifix dangling; each fine-wrought bead
fingered to a dull smoothness,
chain tarnished from handling

but holding firm; I tell my own
blithe and sorry histories, bead after bead,
walk the length of the pier, hands clenched behind my back.

Brüder,
überm Sternenzelt
Muss ein lieber Vater wohnen :

Traveller

One day when we were young
One beautiful morning in May…

A pair of mallard
circled down out of a dark sky
and skidded-splashed onto the surface of the lake;
peat-brown feathers of the she, her oboe-call,
the iridescent emerald of the he, his self-importance;

in the top corner of the wild meadow
suddenly foxes: sun on the red-gold pelts,
vixen-play wary with the fox-cubs' swift
tumble and paw-swipe on the grass, small
piccolo-skreeks and high-barks;

from the house the sound of mother's old Dansette,
a wobbling record, (His Master's Voice),
and Tauber's off-white tenor, the reedy
nasal crooning: 'Roses are blooming in Picardy'.
I had been watching father, the beloved –

turned suddenly hunter –
lift down the sleek and hard-shod rifle,
select a blunt-head gold-red cartridge and slick it
into the breach; I knew the bullet-crack would shatter
fur and flesh and bone and end the music.

*

When I first saw the travellers
they were halted in the shadow of a hill, there
as if birthed out of night;

a caravan, green-drab, with a tarped
dirt-black tent drawn in
under the lifted shafts of a cart;

mute and rangey dogs
scavenged the borders of the camp,
a horse and mule –

crestfallen and watching towards unfathomable places –
stood braced against the day; children
in off-brown smocks were finger-in-mouth and big-eye watchful;

there were stones
set to the wheels of the caravan, for keeping,
lest it off suddenly, and bolt.

When I passed home from school, a thick
unsatisfactory smoke was rising;
the children rooted with the dogs

in the measling chaos of pots and scattered blankets.
At home the adults
prated of violence; they told of stolen

hens and eggs, clothing missing off the lines, told
of night-time forays, bodies slipping through the dark
and making the darkness bleed. Once

the big man, dark-clothed, dark-fleshed, came
obsequious, cajoling, to our back door;
Tauber was singing, from the drawing-room

When they begin the beguine,
it brings back a night of tropical splendour…

the big man
eyed me, and I knew a small,
inexpressible, guilt.

*

I had my own immaculate days of lake and sky
and far-scented bog-sprung hillsides; I had
a crafted tub, rake for mast and sheet for sail;
to bump its prow against the black turf bank

in the sweetest influence of breeze
was all of adventure I then required;
I registered the fox-bark, how it told
a story of fugitive survival, I had found –

where the shore was dangerous
in reed-isle and moss-lawn – a trodden place,
an atrium before a dark lair, and a story-book
of hen-feathers, gristle-spit, and bone-claw. Once

*

I saw him, big-man, traveller, there
along my landing-place against the lake,
he was stooped over, and doing something;
I was scared of his gruff consonants, his black eyes;
I watched, as fox might watch from the archway of his lair,

and when he left I found
shore-stones darkened from a fire, burnt-black sticks
and up against the bank a midden
of eel-heads, eyes open in slime-black skin,
teeth bared and pin-sharp; the water,

amber-beautiful by the shore, became
a slaughter-place where long black eels emerged
from the peat bottom like filaments of mud, whiplash-fast
and slitherful and I heard, in dreams, the laughter
of the travelling man, and his camp's hubbub.

*

Muted trumpets, harp, the quivering strings:
Lonely on a desert breeze, I may wander where I please,
yet I keep on longing, just to rest a while.

They left, the travellers, as if a mist-filled daylight
swallowed them; there were small and ash-grey patches
clumped across the hill, with rags and timbers

and fox-red flitches of things along the thorns;
there were ash-smells and cooked-flesh fat-spills,
grease-puddles, a fungus-stink of oozed mud;

and I found it difficult to hold my place again
in the uneasy light they had left behind, a dusk-light
that kept on glimmering along once-familiar lanes :

Who have Business with the Sea

The truth – the pity – and the truth (Britten, *Peter Grimes*)

Rosary was an entering on a dusk-light world;
Nanna, distressed for her wayward son out
on terrific seas, prayed that the Christ

(asleep perhaps in the stern) might assuage
the waters; you could hear waves crashing,
breakers house-high and higher sounding

down the chimney; the inner wall of the fireplace
was black as the blackest Atlantic night, hung
with the black snow of soot, turf-sparks like stars

against a black sky. I watched the tears make small
trailings down her talcumed cheeks and I prayed, too,
that his craft be stalwart always on those awful seas.

*

He came towards us, staggering as if the platform
heaved; Nanna clutched my arm and I sensed
her ecstasy of dismay.

'Well, donkey-boy,' he called at me
and there was brandy-sickness on his breath;
he jollied on with me, he could not speak with her.

'All flesh is salt,' he said, and I loved him,
traveller, moustachioed and gentle,
seafarer, petrel, dove:

> *There are those who go down to the sea in ships,*
> *who do business in great waters.*

I loved most his sadness and pale eyes
lightly moist, the high hang of his head
as he watched towards something out over the waves;

When the storms come they reel to and fro
they stagger like drunken men
yet in the end he brings them
to their desired haven.

*

And then I heard, where I was hiding in the hedgerow,
a rustling through the ferns and grasses of the drain: fox!
slow-swaggering through the yellow flags, so close
I could make out each russet hair sunburnished. I saw

the long and breathfilled brush ending in a few
dark hairs, king's train, old guardianship; I saw the eye
rounded and sorrowing, a moon-sliver shape of white
gleaming; saw the long tongue lolling

between sharp and yellow-white teeth as if he smiled,
as if he had vanquished all old mankind's traps
to destroy him. I grew still as the roots of the escallonia,
knew a shiver of fellowship and a pang of guilt,

there where I made myself captain and helmsman,
battling the wheel against a wild sou'-wester,
how I leaned heroically on the wind... call me
Ishmael... call me Ahab... call me Peter Grimes.

*

Wind, in from the North Sea, rips like teeth;
Sizewell in the near distance, its dumb
threat, its sheen; on the long and stony sea-front
seagulls hold endless high-toned conversation;

in the old-world spacious graveyard, Aldeburgh,
Britten and Pears are whispering, out of the wind's heave;
Sunday morning, an early winter-grey,
sibilant hush of leaves along the footpath,

the parish church of the Apostles
calls to worship, iterated clamour of the bells
in a music ever-so-slightly off its key;
they lie side by side now, Britten, Pears,

storms ended, where they wish to be,
in their simple graves; everything, save the bells,
in harmony, the waves of grass, the meadowed ocean,
Peter Grimes forever striding down the coast.

*

Traveller, I have come again to sit by the sea,
its many-coloured inks

writing over and over the names and origins and destinations
of its heart-stuffs, its periwinkles, sea-wolves, squid;

all of the dead and living out there
ghost-floating in a world

larger and more violent than our own, whole
cities of them, Philadelphias with Amish country,

wide ocean-Connemaras and pilgrim mountains
where cold-blooded tourist-fish file by

in staring congregations;
so much blood spilt it salts the ocean

and I see things crawl and reach,
slimed creatures spittle-boned and fin-fleshed

out of God's boiling and creating waters,
all of us longing ever for the pacific fields of the Son.

*

'All flesh is salt,' he said, and I loved him. There is a last
photograph in the black-bleak family album; he, child
of his times, wanderer, sea-farer, old

man, stands before a white church
in light-blue suit, white shirt, blue tie,
beside him the quiet woman whom he found

to hold him still in the last years;
he smiles, self-consciously, across oceans
towards Nanna who has long ago found her final stillness.

>   *O tide that waits for no man*
>   *Spare our coasts :*

Bead after Bead

Sicut cervus desiderat… (Palestrina)

Kilshane. The novitiate. A settled
island. After the island. We slowed,
up the long driveway, Nanna already sobbing

with pride, and loss; this, too, part of the dream, priest
in the family, an affirmation. Her
plot, prayed for. *A thaisce… My treasure*: grandfather

gone the way of flesh. I held a small brown suitcase
emptied of childish things, and stood
bemused, in a conservatory, exotic butterflies

throbbing on exotic plants, orchids, African, Brazilian,
and Brother Ambrose keeping the windows shut.
I was to learn lessons in standing still

to allow the day in all its motions be the same
as it was in the beginning, and shall be.
As the deer pants after the founts of water…

*

No photos of grandfather remain
in the family album; we called him 'sir', he was

stern and patriarchal, just like God. He led
rosary at bed-time, bead after bead, circling.

I knelt beside him once in chapel,
proud to be on the men's side, but he kept

nudging me to kneel up straight, stop fidgeting.
I looked up at the Virgin's face where she stood

niched, hands folded; I glanced to see if her eyes
moved, or if she fidgeted out of her boredom.

*

Because, novice to the time, I was part of it,
the harmony, the certitude, the uplift –
because I had traipsed in, from sea-cliffs and sea-roar
to the walled garden of the Song of Songs – I prayed

kindle in me
the fires of holy love; I would
go up in flames and leave
a charred patch on the earth.

*

Now I lay me down to sleep…
I folded my arms over my heart:

prayed: *Oh Lover crucified!* and eased my soul
to a blessed metaphysical darkness, entering

original, essential loneliness. Exhausted
after exercises of the soul I prayed

nunc dimittis servum tuum, Domine…

*

Catch the foxes for us, the little foxes
wreaking havoc in the vineyards
because our vineyards are in flower…

I left the Ireland of forge and country dance-hall,
of braces, corsets, the mission, sin,
and wandered down clerestories in a sacred daze;

it was a question for me then
of putting on the Christ as if he were soutane
and stock and collar, new man, old man, overcoat; relished

the sweet and sensual softnesses of dusk-light,
soothing darkness of trees at the world's edge,
the wood behind us going up in flames;

uncertain where we were, and why,
we sang our hearts out and the lift and sway of the chant
clouded our minds…

*

Nanna, you'd laugh to see me, sometimes, ring the semi-
nary bell announcing angel-time, or festival High Mass. I
have to swing my weight on the long rope, three draws
without a muttering from the bell, building-up, like
preparation for prayer, and then a surge and I'm hoisted
high, the bell calling, I in flight, like Icarus, three times
three and nine, a music ever-so-slightly off its key, but it
brings me back to Bunnacurry grove when I'd climb,
grandchild, among the pine-trees towards the windy top
and sit, part of it, and then the chapel bell would ring the
Angelus and three minutes later the bell from the
monastery would call and I'd see you, there in the yard,
praying, you'd strike your breast and the Word was made
flesh and you'd genuflect and hold yourself, head bowed,
a long time in reflection…

*

Sicut cervus desiderat ad fontes aquarum
ita desiderat anima mea ad te Dominum
We stood, a male enclave, with our male antagonisms,

particular friendships, the low-slung cincture,
the musks, and sang Orlando Lassus, the motets,
and Palestrina, *as the deer pants after living water*... male

harmonies, the resonant and echoing Gregorian
that lifted us out of time and swung us, gratefully,
into the warm dark of the Middle Ages.

*

Jackie, thanks for your always welcome letter. It's as ever good to hear from you, I know you can write only once a month. I take up my pen now to tell you all is well and quiet here, DG. Father Tiernan has complained off the altar about the dance-hall back the road. The monastery in Bunnacurry is being closed. Doesn't that say something about the times that are in it? The foxes have been in the chicken-run again. The travellers are back and are camping just outside the old quarry. I am lonesome, between times. I have not been feeling all that well, pains in my chest, tiredness. Pray for me...

*

She died;
I stood over her plot
in stole and surplice
sprinkling water,
holding myself detached
in sacred ceremony, as if love
could not have scope
and human tears were failure;
Nanna, treasure in heaven;
childhood over
and the dim ages, my eyes
opening.

*

I sat by the ocean's edge, Ogunquit, Maine;
along the coast the Boston summer crowds, the cries,
the urgencies towards the founts of salt water.
I gazed eastwards; over there, thousands of miles,

the island, the old beliefs. Child of that time, who was he?
and the seminarian? do I know him? and those
seasons of ritual, great silences, withdrawal; that
cabin-fever; fox-stink; the cell, comforting, and comfortless :

Writing out the Myth

Locus iste… (Bruckner)

Anton Bruckner, quiet-spoken,
faith-inclined, sat in his drawing-room assembling
harmonies, '*vierstimmigen Chor*' – the pen
is mightier – motets, music

to penetrate the soul with its seduction,
sacred fountains of the love of God: *locus iste*
a Deo factus est inaestimabile sacramentum;
a priceless sacrament…

*

This is the morning flight, the Irish on the move,
different migrations now out over Holyhead;
a still, a scarcely tiding, Irish Sea of clouds

and England's pleasing pasturelands. Take a right
turn south, banking; gleams from a car six miles below;
old Europe, the fabulous, we breaststroke through

blue lakes of air, in over Amsterdam (Anne Frank),
and Leipzig (Bach's *Thomaskirche*), Prague (Franz Kafka)
towards Budapest (Attila József), and at last

– Warsaw, Dresden, should we drift a little to the north –
down the long slope of air into Sofia, new world,
where international wolves of promise

are moving down out of Vitosha's snow-patched peaks.
Then see me rise, in a luxe glass cage with garrulous writers,
on the outside wall of a plush, post-communist, hotel.

*

Father's handwriting was a fishing-line
shivering in the chill air;
it sloped forward, in haste
to catch up on the words

shoaling across his brain;
he left small (*a little book of hours*)
translations, exclamations, tracks,
on the margins of his books so I could hear

the snorting horses of *Taras Bulba*
gallop over the steppes
of Bunnacurry bogs.
Towards the end it was squiggle-writing,

tapering off at last
as if a fly, rambling across spilled blue ink,
had lifted off the paper
into thin air, into pure air, into Word.

*

Sofia: the heavy-set, vast and rough-old-times
Palace of Culture where we come, corralled together
to fret about indifference to our words: heavy-set

serious men and women, Azerbaijan to the USA,
spilling out words like marbles across the boards, bland
agate playthings, the world beyond beyond us.

*

In the beginning I had crayons,
waxy, thick as my father's middle finger;
paper from old brown packaging;

I made lines, my every-which-way
rush across the paper, my marks,
my lightning-flashes, my slug-trails.

Mausoleum hall, Sofia; I return my earpiece and translation set
and make my way to the table, wines and meats, more un-
animated conversation. I have come a long way

from island. Or have I? Afternoon, see us, European
Academy of poetry, Luxembourg, Slovakia, handling
strange languages in tangle-weeds of words.

*

I had a slate before me on the desk
where I slid in,
short pants, short legs; a pristine finger

of white chalk.
I made a line, waverful, a scratching,
like hens; Mrs Kilbane applauded:

'you have written – I!'
I had a pen, at a big desk, a brass sliding-lid
over a depthless well of sea-blue ink,

there was a headline copybook: *Pim*
put a bib on Bab with a pin:
and soon it would be joined-up

writing; I would be part of it, a link in the Altamira chain
through Achill Island
to Zimbabwe. The word. The Word. Traveller.

Linked signs, in order,
like vine-rows on the hills of Aquitaine,
like fence posts

driven down to keep the lifestock safe.
I still write down the word
with the same, waverful

scratching sound, knowing
I have never got it right, the pronoun,
the word: 'I'.

*

Off the marsh road, a flock of stray and vagrant
high-stepping cranes, grave demoiselles, has been moving
in slow ballet across the wet

as if the earth on which they deigned to walk
were tarnished, tarnishing and giving life. They have become
travellers, winds taking them from their natural

environment. We know, too, how storms take us, set us down
on unknown territory where we grasp for hold.
Paul, the apostle, told how he was lifted off the earth

and into Paradise, discovering things of which
no-one might speak;
I have been listening now, for decades; moments

when I achieve a sacred quiet, I have heard
with Bruckner, Elgar, Brahms, harmonies
beyond listening; I have been offered words and set

them down, relishing a slow, muted applause –
yours John Donne, George Herbert's, yours,
Hopkins, and yours, Andrew Marvell. I listen

where the full-dressed poplar down by the red gate
sashays silkily in its obligation; I set it down
defiantly, in your shadow, Dickinson, at your side, Smart.

Mist this morning on the still grasses. The spiders' webs
– slight as dream-catchers – scarcely visible
on bush and heather, shiver

wispfully in the no-breeze; an old man, gaunt
in the inheritance of famine, has lost his son
to the murk of a canal and walks his rush-snagged fields,

in silence, eyes dulled as daub. I am relearning
ignorance so I may write foolishly again and say
it will be all right, it will be all

right; we carry inside our flesh the bones
of the death of the Lord Jesus
and on our shoulder-blades the nubs

of spirit-wings. Paul
could never tell for sure, whether his flight
was in or out of body. And always

Icarus stands aggrieved, waxwings raised
in preparation for the myth, listening for the breeze
that will lift him out of flesh into the gorgeous sun.

*

At our conference the big men listen
to their own voices, voices that say
I am big, important, cover my chest

with medals, then walk behind me
at a respectful distance; dark-clothed,
dark-fleshed, and aggrieved, sophisticated men.

*

In his drawing-room, Anton Bruckner sat,
wearied, knowing
his *Symphony No. 9 in D Minor*

would not be finished;
he was sitting by the window, allowing darkness;
a few last rooks

crossed, black against grey, towards the wood;
he was there not-there, thinking
how his symphony might close with a chorus –

Freude, D Major,
like his master's – how he had worked to put
the self-rending God

together again:
all the king's horses, all the king's men…
He laughed, his own *Te Deum*

ranging through his mind.
Now, about his grave, mother-of-pearl dragonflies
are shivering in sunlight.

*

Traveller, there remains
a heart-light, one
you will not declare at the borders,
nor flash (*locus iste*)
at passport control: your will to live

justly, without despair,
your will to offer
mercy, to accept forgiveness,
your will to walk
with hope, without expectation, in the shadow

of your urgent God
and to express, in the moments
offered to you on this one and insulated day,
the messages from on high
you have been entrusted to translate :

Pastoral Symphony

and in my flesh shall I see God... (Handel)

They step beside you, the faithful ones,
tapping you on the shoulder with fingers of air,

writing to you –
in rediscovered postcards – of avenues in the sun,

blessing you with the useless gifts, the souvenirs
you hesitate to throw away.

They grow animated as you approach the field
beneath whose heathers they have, for a season,

vanished – like orchids among the downland grasses –
twayblade, for example, with its small musk-scented flowers,

or helleborine, white lady, with its nectar, its fragrances.
They will lie, the ruined bodies,

waiting, in the scraped earth, under JCB and rubble,
but will lift again, in original beauty, in a new season. Now

it is Ireland, and summer, though fields and rain
make dismal harmonies; I, too,

am of Ireland, its dirge and requiem, its adagio;
I have tried to find

wild-meadow oratorios that might offer yet
heart-warming clarities. Like Handel,

who came, in a darker age, to write something
for the Dublin poor, and offered them *Messiah*,

in the Musick Hall, Fishamble Street, the ladies
to come without hoops, the gentlemen

without swords, so he could find scope
for the Christ-birth pastoral, and for the lift

of a *Hallelujah!* We walked the commonage
– where skylarks trilled over marsh and heathland –

in search of orchid; the brow of bare Ben Bulben
stood in the distance

with sunlight passing across
like a herd of emerald horses;

and I have been wondering
about the usefulness of poetry,

if it is eucharist, to consume and be consumed.
Handel gave to the words

a music of troubling grace: *we shall be changed,*
in a moment, in the twinkling of an eye – though the Christ

is not yet substance of the earth, nor is humankind
coherent to the extent of love. Child

of the times I seek
orchid-faithfulness to the tasking poetry of spirit

while they step beside me still, the faithful ones
and tip me on the shoulder with their asking fingers of air :

As Breath against the Windowpane

veni, Sancte Spiritus… (William Byrd)

Breath.
The life-gift, and its gracious
taking away.

Red vestments, the spirit-colour, festival;
Spiritans, soldiers of the Holy Ghost,
we rose in choir to chant, *veni Sancte Spiritus…*

and inhaled, deeply; ours the Paraclete, gift
of the most high God. Surplices like snow. Soutanes
scarlet, like the holly-berry, red as blood.

*

I remember nothing of it, I being
just birthed out of the waters; but she was there,
the beautiful young woman already inhaling
death, and the grey-suited man who had now
taken his chemistry degree. Breath measureless
before me. They say I started out of comfort,

and screeched in protest, that dribble of cold
water, the scorch of chrism. They say the white
shawl they wrapped me in was lifted back
exposing me to the cleansing, my intaken breath
drawing fire out of the air into my bones.
Naming me flesh. And blood. Spirit. And clay.

*

What would you have seen, had you
been there? That other baptism. There was a river,

shallow in that place, you hear its waters
carolling softly over stones; there were trees

merciful in the heat, olive trees perhaps, their limbs
contorted; valleys sloped away on either bank; the flowing,

the mystery and message of stepping in, a sense
that downriver are all the washed-out dead; too much

heaviness, and too much pain; your feet
hurting on the stones. You wished, then, as often since,

for cleansing, to start again, your fretted skin
carried downstream, your many sadnesses carried too.

Then there is that Stranger, standing sure
in his raked flesh, eyes focused on your soul

willing to draw it out? And the sky rent suddenly,
opening for a moment on a world

green beyond the blue, with strange birds circling
and all the washed-out dead

swaying together like water-reeds, voices
so loud you could not hear them till he, the Stranger

stumbling in the wash beside you, reaches out
for help, and holds you, eyes green and cruel,

then turns as if called to shore and begins
to trek away into ungainable distance. You

have become, since then, a traveller, following.

*

Byrd's Ordinary of the Mass: those crying voices,
the instruments, for instance, for the *sanctus*:
duet for fox and hunting horns, air

on the wolf-string: *Kyrie
eleison*... Lord, have mercy,
Kyrie, Christe, Kyrie.

*

You stepped out that evening, your hand
in your father's hand; your breathing
shaped infant ghosts upon the air; frost
haled across the fields and heathlands

a chill and feather-delicate scattering of white;
the night was cold, cloudless, and when you stood
up on the quarry hill you saw the village
breathless in expectation, a candle lit

in every window while all the sky was rife
with candlelights; you still held tight
to your father's hand, the silence
grown between you more companionable;

you stood, awed, peace
levelling all your senses so that when you set
homewards you were big with love, you danced
on stars that sang hosanna in each frosted-over pool.

*

I am one, now, of an eldering congregation
bearing the burden of failing bodies;
even the mind, at times, is a scattering of leaves
across the winds; widows and widowers dealing yet again
with solitude; pain in our pockets, awareness
of the sharpening indignities. But we light –
to the old familiar words – the first

purple candles of the season, his passion now
closer and most certain. We stoop in fellowship
of the unknown Spirit, skirting bitterness, inhaling faith;
inclined to a childish kind of braggadocio designed
to fool, and to sustain; a curious fellowship, this disturbed
awareness of breathing. Before our eyes the flight
of a stained-glass dove across a stained-glass sky.

*

The body motionless on its marble slab, the air
in the dark room thick with whisperings:
the sound the candle-flames make as they dip and bow
holding their places on the standards round the coffin's

commanding presence. I stand, breathless; there is that
cannot be spoken in words – whereby the Word is spoken.
Reed birds swinging to the reeds' swing
in a sibilance scarce this side of silence.

Listen: the spittering of needle-perfect rodent-legs
through the turf-mould grits of the abandoned shed.
Listen: through the dark night the chandelier
retains the shivering – Byrd's *Four-Part Mass*: *dona*

nobis pacem: ... you may hear it
vibrating still in glass-contained excitement :

Night on Skellig Michael

Dream Vision of the Peasant Lad... (Mussorgsky)

The small half-decker smelled of fish-blood and old oils;
the engine sputtered, died, then caught, a cough
of black smoke lifted towards the quay. Grey day, though calm
in the lee of land, but the waves and wash demanding

out on the open sea. Lift
and fall, sidelong
sluice, splashing of spray over the bow, loll and pitch
of the deck –

made me hold hard to the gunwale, its varnished and rounded
                                                        wood
rough now as an aged hand. I was
temporal, temporary seafarer, traveller, legs braced,
with an assumed bravado.

It is a getting away, and a getting to. Skelligs, extreme
islands, far out to sea; strict and overwhelming, dark-walled
                                                        bastion.
The skipper scattered bread from his sandwich
to the white horses of the sea: you make offerings, he grinned,

to the god that keeps you. A herring gull
flipped its body over, swooped, and caught; I saw
its yellow bill with that small bloodberry, and its yellow eye
watchful. Atlantic patient then in the Blue Cove; Skellig

Michael, wild and furious as that high archangel
who holds the entrance to the heart of God. Roots of the island
claw down into the fiery entrails of the earth,
mother-mountain, sacrament and threat. Awed

I began up the steep black steps
broken out of the ribs of rock, tripped, almost at once, my palm
scraping on a loose shingle, drops of blood
an early offering to the island. Looming

above me, the torturous climb, up towards shadow.
Difficult, and tasking. I turned, often, to rest,
to watch out over the Atlantic, breath
taken by the wind-touched silences, save

where the squabbling of kittiwakes on the cliff walls
spoke the cacophonies of ego-bickering; no
delicate harmonies here, no soft-pedalling, no mute.
Thought of Mussorgsky, *Night on Bald Mountain*: the witches'

sabbath. I sweated, stomach heaved with effort, not as young...
I paused to see the tiny growths along rock walls, there
as if they have clung forever: sea-campion, hawkbit,
prickly cowthistle, pearlwort. I reached, wearied,

*

the longed-for monastery at the rough-hewn edge
of heaven, at the sensuous ridge of Hell; the silent
abandoned praying-places, stone crosses

pitted by gales, the rounded skulls of eremite cells
creased by winter storms, spring tempests; lurking-nest
of the suffering soul, Mussorgsky, Ishmael, Ahab, Grimes...

*

I stood a long time, shivering, summer, with the chill
of height and evening wind, with old disturbances

long settled in the dust under my feet. House of those
who lost their lives to win them back. The poem,

as the hermits did, raddles its being to find the soul:
source and sustenance, summit, Spirit, end. I found

*

shelter inside a cell, took from my rucksack
bread and whiskey, made of them my Eucharist, calling
on the Christ-name, my edible, drinkable God,

and knew my flesh and earth-flesh
suffused with the blood of Jesus. I lay down
on hard clay, and tried to sleep. Turned,

hurting, earth cold beneath me,
storm-petrel, shearwater
whispering their way into burrow and crevasse underground.

I turned at last into old darkness, Jesus
in the bloodstream, dreamed
Eucharist of old saints, of anchorite, eremite, and was in tune.

*

Woke again, head hurting and body sore.
Horizons were touched with light

and all about the sea-birds soared and cried; I breakfasted,
bread, and a redeeming draught of whiskey. Down

at the landing place I sat
and waited; through mist-filled daylight heard

the throbbing engine of a boat... All flesh, I thought,
is stone, is water... I had been, and would be

part of it, pain and prayer, rock and guano-white cliff-ledges;
would touch again the universal Christ,

the urgency, exemplar and the ground, Christ
the truth, the pity, and the truth :

Mother and Child

You, God's flowers, lily white,
blossom on, you flowers of May
that my son, my beloved,
may sleep on peacefully.

(Henryk Górecki, *Symphony of Sorrowful Songs*)

Father spoke of Poland, of the girl who wrote
prayers on the wall of a cell
while the war of wars
went unabated. In December 1943 there were men

in Europe, falling on the soiled-snow battlegrounds,
flailing their arms
as if they would fashion out
snow-angels, who were jerking into stillness while the snow

covered them, only their hands lifting, their fingers
pointing. In a hospital, in the easy west,
a man stooped over a wicker cot
and gathered in his arms the white body

of his new-born son. Sometimes I feel the shiver of his wonder
as one small hand
closes about his finger,
my eyes shut, my being still shaking from the sweetness

of womb-cream, the rolling of the ever-shifting tides
of the eternal, my other hand
a fist, readying myself
for the battle, angered at my sudden, irretrievable loss.

*

One can say, in music, what cannot be said
when the forces of political oppression
are scourges through the fields and streets; there is
Palestine, and Syria, Iraq... and then there is

Poland, the Warsaw Philharmonic, the slow
ponderous movements of the sacred spirit,
double bass to cello to viola to mother's voice,
sorrowful songs achieving passionate calm:

Mamo, nie płacz, nie.	*Mother, don't weep, don't.*
Niebios Przeczysta Królowo,	*Most holy Queen of Heaven*
Ty zawsze wspieraj mnie.	*Help me now and always.*
Zdrowa Mario	*Ave Maria*

*

Dear, dead, Father:
        I have put Górecki's *3rd Symphony*
in the player; *sostenuto tranquilo ma cantabile*;
I see the mother's arms folded round her Son,
she rocks, slowly, over, back, in, out, the grief

rampant in the basses, this hopeless circling, mothers
against crucifixion: *Son, chosen and beloved one,*
let your mother share your wounds… I feel
despair oppressing me, the beauty of the songs

uplifting. When will we ever…? Will humankind…?
Mornings (do you remember?) opening
in delirious expectation the old stable door,
this day's light slanting in across last night's crop

of the whitest baby-tops, lifting themselves off the hot
and fragrant compost, reeking of horse.
In the darkened shed they spread themselves along,
a sanctity, graced by husbandry and night. Picked,

they came from the root with a hurt squeak and were ranged
in perfect order in the baskets, that precious whiteness
only the black of night can prosper, that hard-soft skin
resistant but nicked too easily to expose

the light-gold ribs; Pray, they urged in their regulated rows,
for us sinners, now and at the hour... like white
coffins of the children, Omagh, Srebrenica and Iran,
Angola, Kosovo, Israeli murders in the Lebanon...

*

The red spot on the kitchen wireless
flickered;
there were whistling sounds, disturbances, they said,
from winds that blow
everywhere across the face of earth;

grandfather
leaned close, one big hand cupped to one big ear;
a polished voice came quavering
and fell away, flowed back, something about
the Korean war, atrocities, advances, the mounting

numbers of the slain; nothing new, the old man said, and spat
expertly on the fire.
Outside
trees were scuffling in an ever-present seashore dissonance;
I pressed my face to the window,

water-dribbles on the pane, and all the world beyond
was worried into breaking
patterns.
I crept upstairs again, to the bulked
and brass-hasped trunk; beneath the folded, mothballed

old-sheets and lace cloths of Nanna's keeping, I found
the jacket of his uniform, peaked cap
with harp
and crown insignia and I marched
down-up, down-up, an RIC cadet, imagined pistols

manly on my hip. When I came down
grandfather was watching the labouring of the flames,
moist sods shifting as they burned; with a sigh
he settled back
and touched the dark-brown splotches on his wrist.

*

Ah, you wicked, wicked men
in the name of God most holy
why, oh why, have you killed
my son?

*

Dear Emily Maria,

We have learned how to bring the sky down, we are expert
at altering the weather and flinging our debris
against the face of Mars –

and we reached, in our time, zero point at 9/11
and where were we to go from there? down
minus? or take the first impossible step

towards the abolition of all wars?
The lamentation reads: *Because, dear son,*
I have carried you ever closer to my heart

and served you ever faithfully, speak
now to your mother, give her happiness, though already
you are leaving me, you, my hope, my cherished hope;

Emily, it goes on, from within the human heart…

Now you are four months old, and lie
peaceful in your mother's arms; Emily, there exists
unquestioning love, the wide-armed

all-embracing care of the Christ-man.

Alle Menschen werden Brüder   *All people will be brothers*
Wo Dein sanfter Flügel weilt   *Where your tender wing lingers*

*

The monastery offered him cadavers, he would sculpt for them
a body crucified, shaping the cavity of a chest
strained into contortions, the scaffolding of the ribs

skewed against awful suffering; he would sculpt
long fingers of the Madonna, white flesh
of the Christ. He had learned how the belly

is rounded out, and would sculpt a Bacchus, grapes for hair,
the flaccid serpent-stump yet idle, or cherubs
ripe with wisdom, and pubescent; marks of the chisel

a fleshly signature; awakening slave, a work
unfinished. More telling, so. Shadows are born
from the constant striking on the stone that makes

flesh flesh, and look! in spite of bone he knows
we are nursling spirits, grace-filled, and may soar!
That the killings stop, that the desecration of bodies

stop! Michelangelo has been, has left us David, the Pietà :

An Eldering Congregation

That masterful negation and collapse
Of all that makes me man... (Elgar, *Dream of Gerontius*)

I am confronted now with the weight of body
and the spirit's blank, half-willed ascendancy;
in the dark night I wake, uncertain if the sounds I've heard
are insinuations from the dead, or smallest creatures scurrying

somewhere between slates and ceiling. Sleep
is not won easily; dreams recur, old arguments, futilities;
vision blurs and memory has become a marshy bog; to you I pray –
Jesus, old fox and clever-paws, old wily-snout – deal

gently with me now. High tide by afternoon, Atlantic
purring like a tom cat under sun, swollen moment of plenitude
before the turn. The years, taking on themselves
the fortitude of dreams, have been passing swift as dreams; my hair

holds like tufts of fine bog-cotton, skin crinkles
like the gold of gutter-leaves; the ribs of splayed half-deckers
are the days of my well-loved dead cluttering my own low tides;
whether my fall is to be hard or I'm to drift away under white

soft-billowing sails, I would that they could say of me, yes
he lived, and while he lived
he gathered a few, though precious, poems
lacquered with brittle loveliness, like shells.

*

Nicolai Gedda is singing from the front room:

> *Sanctus fortis, Sanctus Deus,*
> *De profundis oro te,*
> *Miserere, Judex meus,*
> *Parce mihi, Domine.*

It is high summer in Ireland, and darkness grows
mid-morning, rain
falling, the meadows
sorry-looking, passing trucks raise muddy spray;

> *Go forth upon thy journey, Christian soul!*
> *Go from the world! Go, in the name of God...*

evening, tractors in the fields are in a rush
for harvest,
the green hay
baled and wrapped in black plastics, crossed in white chalk

against the crows; Gerontius, old man, having died,
begins a new journey
and Elgar's music –
chorus of souls – catches the old dread, the terror:

> *Go forth upon thy journey, Christian soul!*
> *Go from the world! Go, in the name of God...*

*

Grandfather, in his last months,
took to sitting in a fireside chair, contemplating

the shifting turves, the ash
filtering itself soundlessly down; he'd stand, at times

to knock the bowl of his pipe
against the grate, take slow minutes with the plug, rubbing it

in his dried palms, inhaling
with satisfaction. Sometimes he'd rise, sighing, make

unsteady way to the workshop,
memory of old excitement stirring him, and stand

watching in amongst dim workspaces,
gazing at his fingers as if there was something he had lost.

He disappeared upstairs, then,
and the house hushed.

Now his grave, in the island cemetery,
is a riot of neglect, long bramble-vines and grasses taking hold;

rushes and meadow-sweet
flourish in the wet-daub acres of the field;

rain falls along the stones, lichen
eats away the histories, the names, the century.

*

> *Firmly I believe, and truly*
> *God is three and God is one,*
> *And I next acknowledge duly*
> *Manhood taken by the Son…*

*

You may step off the old stone pier
onto rocks at the ocean's edge, over boulders,
salt-braced rocks, erratics; the sea idling, long

arms of kelp sashaying in the swell;
you may be part of something, between-wheres, between-times,
the distant islands shrouded,

the inland meadows dulled. In soft
off-the-Atlantic and persistent mists, you will stand
absorbed, flesh-heavy, anticipating spirit-shapes

and their whisperings as they pass, incautiously, by;
up on the mountain road the toiling
engine of a truck is an intrusion

yet a strong lien holds you to the invisible
and almost-visible, while you are relishing
the all-embracing ovoid bone-structuring

of the earth. Too soon this solitary existence
will have become so exquisite you will call
out urgently for companionship.

*

And father, the strict one, faith-inclined,
stood, in his final months to lean against a boulder
on Keem Strand, his body red and blotched
after a swim; he was shivering in a wind that swept

in off the Atlantic though he held himself erect,
eyes watching out over the bay to the wild horses
of the ocean. He moved, at last, in under the shelter
of a cliff, out of the world-wind, to light

his cigarette; small pools waited at the roots of rocks
for the tide that would swell them into seas;
dunlins raced along the lace edgings of the waves;
high over Croghaun grey clouds moved by; I believe

his mind hung heavily on sorrows. He, too, disappeared
into pure air, into Word, and into these, my words.

*

I sit in church, one of an eldering congregation;
umpteenth Sunday in ordinary time; the lector reads
St Paul, Letter to the Romans: creation still retains

the hope of being freed, as we do, from this slavery
to decadence... And there they are, kneeling
and motionless, two pews ahead of me, on the men's side,

grandfather, father, upright and straight, their beads
rattling gently against the bench-wood, like the insistent
regular tap–tap–tap of a metronome; I pray

Agnus Dei, then *Domine non sum dignus*; then rise into the line
behind them up to the altar-rails, to share the bread, the wine,
to speak consent to the world and to its Christ :

Snow Falling on Chestnut Hill

Denn alles Fleisch es ist wie Gras… (Brahms)

It is late now in the day; that curving lane
with grass and plantain, clovers and pimpernels
forming a hump along the centre, seems
to be straightening towards a conclusion. I have arrived

in a strange city, evening; (I am hearing
Brahms, the *German Requiem*, *Selig sind…* blessed
are they who mourn.)
Boston. A big house, and daunting.

They have warned me of arctic chill
reaching this way, over Canada, the Lakes, Chicago;
Herr, lehre doch mich… I have heard already
oboe-moans through the eldering house, thin

reed-sounds through unseen interstices: O Lord
make me aware of my last end.
The hollow spaces of the house
are stirred along their dust: All flesh, the music tells,

is grass. I listened, dozing gently, silence
encompassing, engaging me;
at the front door I heard…
(no matter, it is no matter). I stood

watching first snowflakes
visible against the street-lamps; there was the feel
as of the breathing on my face of a lover, as of the brush
of a kiss, sheer

arctic salt, a hosting. *Wir haben hier
keine bleibende Stadt…*
All flesh
is snow. And snow

does not abide. *Selig sind die Toten*, blessed
are the dead; they are at rest
in the Lord's hands. I slept
fitfully; strange

land, strange house, strange dreams; time
raddling me. I could hear
the sound of the deepest night
lying still under a delicate coming down of snow.

*

I have been wondering
about our blizzards of pain and agony – Lupus, for instance,
immune systems down and civil war along the blood.
Prance of the alpha wolf. Bone

scaffolding showing through.
I lay, restless; my temporary home
whispered to itself in house-language, its wooden shifts
of consonants, its groaning vowels, when there came (Christ!)

a sudden rapping
against the door. I listened. Again,
rapping, urgent. I crept down. Opened,
I had to, street door, screen door. Saw

darkness active out there, snow
swirling, a shape that
formed and faded out of the skirl of white and grey…
And she came, breathless,

shaking snow from her hair and face, stomping her feet,
stood in the non-light of the hallway and snow
pooled about her shoes. She, dressed in white,
reached to drop – 'a gift,' she said – one

bright Christmas rose, helleborus,
white-petalled, dark green-leaved,
across the hallstand.
'You!' I whispered. 'You?'

She smiled.
'But we laid you down decades ago,' I said, 'to rest.'
'Isn't it good,' she said,
'to hear the crunch, under your feet, of fresh snow?'

'You are... in body, then?' 'Soul
and body, body and soul. No longer flawed.
I passed where snow is a swarm of whitest butterflies
though I had been growing old with the wolves.'

'And why? Why now? And how...?'
'I bring,' she answered, 'gifts. Wolves, too, wolves'
she whispered, 'wolves are the lambs of God.'
'Our child,' I tried, 'is wrapped up tight in pain, God's ways...'

> (I saw, then, the wolf-pack, *canis lupus*, settling under trees,
> they lie easy in the snow, you can hear their howl-songs, clar-
> inet-calls off-key in the moon-enlightened night, drawn-out
> off-melodies, lauds chanted to the blood, their green-lit
> white-shaded eyes sweeping across the heavens; *canis lupus*,
> grey-grizzled ancients of days, the black, the white, the
> gorgeous fur and in the distance I heard the freight-train howl
> of human hungers, a tailed-off threatening horn-call across
> the night; wolf-pelt, winter-pelt, the scars, the tissues, and
> always snow falling down the everyvein of air)

'Be peacefilled now,' she said, softly as a brushing-by of snow,
'it is late, my traveller, live at peace in the rush
of arctic wind. We are all
sunlight, dimmed, all snowfall, thawed.'

'Our child…'
But she was already moving towards the door, her head
shaking; 'All flesh is snow,
snow-fox, snow-pelt I have been, with you,

a lover, singing against the moon,
a lamb…' The door… I felt the touch of pre-dawn frost,
heard snow in its soft slide, its fistfuls from the trees,
'Wolves, too,' she said, 'wolves

are the lambs of God'.
'Wait!' I called, and reached
for her. But she was gone,
suddenly, and there was nothing, 'I have

questions… prayers…'
Silence, only, and absence. I heard still
the breathing of the snow, a car somewhere
climbing a hill. I stood in darkness. Stood. Perplexed,

as always. A snow-plough passed, the steel blades
scraping against the roads. Soon
cars, roof-racked with snow, would shift
like herds of caribou

down the long parkway. The first
faint light of a new day
touched the window. I saw,
on the hallstand, fresh and beautiful,

one hellebore, one Christmas rose.
I closed my eyes against the dawn and heard
Brahms again: *Wie lieblich sind die Wohnungen…*
how beautiful your dwellings, Lord, how beautiful :

Coda

Laudate Dominum... (Mozart)

for Emily Maria

The Joseph lilies swayed and Tauber sang
one beautiful morning in May while we lit
white candles for your birthing,

and I remembered

how I had danced, midnight, in the street,
iris in the gardens like hallelujahs!
your mother born.

*

We flew to you, out over Holyhead,
to Amsterdam, its high-necked, building-block houses,
where Anne Frank lived with her secrecies,
where swallows are flying low

over the waters of the canal; it was told
in school she shielded her writing with her hands, as I did,
the wonder of it, the solitude.

We passed towards you, by houseboats
with their flowerpots, their cats, with twisted bicycle wheels
in the murk of the water and then! I held you,
so small you might break in my arms, your fist, perfect,

curled to my finger and all the ancestors
crowded round, and all posterity, and they danced,
all of them, their furious dance, there on the head of a pin –

Freude!

*

Grandfather was a self-made carpenter, his long hands
always tender towards the wood; in my eyes
he was always big, always old; he trod the earth
beyond me, a rock of being, heavy with authority;

but he, too, slipped away into a dust-hung corner
of memory, is now as if he had not been. I watched him
carve and shape and plane, urging recalcitrant wood
into polished sideboard, tallboy, chair; I knew

I too wanted to be maker, head down over the slate,
hands shielding, seeking, urging recalcitrant words.

*

I listen, while holding
your warm and yielding flesh,

to Mozart's body-shaking music, the rich soprano voice
of Barbara Hendricks, listen! *Laudate Dominum*, because

love exists, and glory beyond our petty flesh,
our grubby hands, our murky secrecies.

*

I would tell you of the moose,
poor creature, bigger and darker than I expected,
sprawled in death on the roadside; of her long,
ungainly head splittered with blood,

her swollen belly peppered with ticks, dung
oozing onto the road; breezes that early morning
were stilled across the birches,

there were slopes of snow
glistering on the White Mountains; a truck, perhaps,
in the chaos of speed and light and thundering... but I find
no words now to tell the particular sorrow

of that spring morning, the trees
budding, the creeks swelling. Because, Emily, listen!
it is Mozart, and she is singing it again:

Laudate Dominum omnes gentes,
laudate Eum omnes populi :

*

One day you may sit
bemused

to work your way into the music of these lines;
you will find me here, should you care to,

who will have long gone rambling, to dance with the ancestors
on the head of that same, old-fashioned pin.

*

These words I write, Emily Maria, are coda;
it is morning in the world again, red fox morning,
you the reprise, and I the dying fall;

on your lips the trace of mother's milk, on your flesh
scent of the talcum of eternity and in the corner of your eye
the preparation of your tear-ducts;
passage of trams outside the window, iron-heavy, sparks

overhead, the drift of spores like thistle-down migrations,
wool-gatherings on the floor of air; higher still
the trails of jets, travellers, skylines, shifting off to take their place
along the clouds; rabbits at their slow hip-hop

by the runway's edges at Schiphol; and listen! the *Ninth*
Symphony, harmonies lifting into joy, *Freude!*
out of the bleak black soil of the earth :

Brüder,
überm Sternenzelt
muss ein lieber Vater wohnen!